3 4028 08125
HARRIS COUNTY PUBLIC LIL

D1000722

Bloom's Modern Critical Interpretations

The Adventures of Huckleberry Finn

The Age of Innocence

Alice's Adventures in Wonderland

All Quiet on the Western Front

Animal Farm

Antony and Cleopatra

The Awakening

The Ballad of the Sad Café

Beloved

Beowulf

Black Boy

The Bluest Eye

Brave New World

The Canterbury Tales

Cat on a Hot Tin Roof

Catch-22

The Catcher in the Rye

The Chronicles of Narnia

The Color Purple

Crime and Punishment

The Crucible

Cry, the Beloved Country

Darkness at Noon

Death of a Salesman

The Death of Artemio Cruz

The Diary of Anne Frank

Don Quixote

Emerson's Essays

Emma

Fahrenheit 451

A Farewell to Arms

Frankenstein

F. Scott Fitzgerald's Short Stories

The Glass Menagerie

The Grapes of Wrath

Great Expectations

The Great Gatsby

Gulliver's Travels

Hamlet

Heart of Darkness

The House on Mango Street

I Know Why the Caged Bird Sings

The Iliad

Invisible Man

Jane Eyre

John Steinbeck's Short Stories

The Joy Luck Club

J.D. Salinger's Short Stories

Julius Caesar

The Jungle

King Lear

Long Day's Journey into Night

Lord of the Flies

The Lord of the Rings

Love in the Time of Cholera

Macbeth

The Man Without Qualities

Mark Twain's Short Stories

The Merchant of Venice

The Metamorphosis

A Midsummer Night's Dream

Miss Lonelyhearts

Moby-Dick

My Ántonia

Native Son

Night

1984

The Odyssey

Oedipus Rex

The Old Man and the Sea

On the Road

One Flew over the Cuckoo's Nest

One Hundred Years of Solitude

Othello

Persuasion

Portnoy's Complaint

Pride and Prejudice

Ragtime

The Red Badge of Courage

Romeo and Juliet

The Rubáiyát of Omar Khayyám

The Scarlet Letter

A Separate Peace

Silas Marner

Slaughterhouse-Five

Song of Solomon

The Sound and the Fury

The Stranger

A Streetcar Named Desire

Sula

The Sun Also Rises

The Tale of Genji

A Tale of Two Cities

"The Tell-Tale Heart" and Other Stories

The Tempest

Their Eyes Were Watching God

Things Fall Apart

The Things They Carried

To Kill a Mockingbird

Ulysses

Waiting for Godot

The Waste Land

Wuthering Heights

Young Goodman Brown

Bloom's Modern Critical Interpretations

J.D. Salinger's
Short Stories

Edited and with an introduction by
Harold Bloom
Sterling Professor of the Humanities
Yale University

BLOOM'S
LITERARY CRITICISM
An Infobase Learning Company

Bloom's Modern Critical Interpretations: J.D. Salinger's Short Stories

Copyright © 2011 by Infobase Publishing
Introduction © 2011 by Harold Bloom

Bloom's Literary Criticism
An imprint of Infobase Publishing
132 West 31st Street
New York NY 10001

Library of Congress Cataloging-in-Publication Data

J.D. Salinger's short stories / edited and with an introduction by Harold Bloom.
    p. cm. — (Bloom's modern critical interpretations)
Includes bibliographical references and index.
ISBN 978-1-60413-272-4 (hardcover)
1. Salinger, J. D. (Jerome David), 1919–2010—Criticism and interpretation.
I. Bloom, Harold.
PS3537.A426Z673 2011
813'.54—dc22

                          2011007901

Bloom's Literary Criticism books are available at special discounts when purchased in bulk quantities for businesses, associations, institutions, or sales promotions. Please call our Special Sales Department in New York at (212)967-8800 or (800)322-8755.

You can find Bloom's Literary Criticism on the World Wide Web at
http://www.infobaselearning.com

Contributing editor: Pamela Loos
Cover design by Alicia Post
Composition by IBT Global, Troy NY
Cover printed by Yurchak Printing, Landisville PA
Book printed and bound by Yurchak Printing, Landisville PA
Date printed: August 2011
Printed in the United States of America

10 9 8 7 6 5 4 3 2 1

This book is printed on acid-free paper.

All links and Web addresses were checked and verified to be correct at the time of publication. Because of the dynamic nature of the Web, some addresses and links may have changed since publication and may no longer be valid.

Contents

Editor's Note   vii

Introduction   1
    Harold Bloom

Seymour: A Clarification   5
    Gordon E. Slethaug

Seymour's Suicide Again: A New Reading of
    J. D. Salinger's "A Perfect Day for Bananafish"   21
    Gary Lane

A Cloister of Reality: The Glass Family   29
    James Lundquist

Salinger Criticism and "The Laughing Man":
    A Case of Arrested Development   53
    Richard Allan Davison

Sergeant X, Esmé, and the Meaning of Words   69
    John Wenke

J. D. Salinger's Religious Pluralism: The Example
    of *Raise High the Roof Beam, Carpenters*   79
    Dennis L. O'Connor

"Along this road goes no one":
    Salinger's "Teddy" and the Failure of Love   95
    Anthony Kaufman

New Light on the Nervous Breakdowns of
        Salinger's Sergeant X and Seymour Glass   107
    Eberhard Alsen

Salinger's *Nine Stories*: Fifty Years Later   115
    Dominic Smith

Chronology   125

Contributors   127

Bibliography   129

Acknowledgments   133

Index   135

Editor's Note

The nine essays gathered here provide a conspectus of the shorter fiction by the author of *The Catcher in the Rye*.

My introduction ventures an estimate of Salinger's actual achievement, which seems to me inflated by popular reception. At eighty-one I may be too old to judge Salinger, yet he measures poorly against his prime precursors, Scott Fitzgerald and Mark Twain. There is also the burden of pretentiousness: Quotations from Kierkegaard, Kafka, and Rilke glare out at the reader from Salinger's text.

The largest difficulty stems from Salinger's religiosity, an odd blend of Zen and Emerson and of other strands as well.

Gordon E. Slethaug attempts to clarify Seymour's "saintliness" and its relation to his suicide, a crux taken up again by Gary Lane and then expanded into a Glass family overview by James Lundquist.

Juxtaposing "The Laughing Man" with its critics, Richard Allan Davison suggests a link between the sorrows of a child's development and the Eastern transcendentalism that overwhelmed Salinger.

A shrewd essay by John Wenke rightly praises "For Esmé—With Love and Squalor," perhaps Salinger's finest story. Whether his religious concerns ever again allowed Salinger such aesthetic freedom is the implicit concern of the other essays in this collection, starting with Dennis L. O'Connor's exegesis of the "religious pluralism" that oddly blends together Emerson and T.S. Eliot, Walt Whitman and Vedanta, Taoism and Thoreau.

Anthony Kaufman valiantly attempts to redeem Salinger's "Teddy," after which Eberhard Alsen returns us to the breakdowns that are a feature of Salinger's art.

The volume concludes with Dominic Smith's backward glance at the *Nine Stories*, praised for their commendable austerity.

HAROLD BLOOM

Introduction

I open by contrasting two passages from Salinger's *Nine Stories:*

> Less than a minute later, Esmé came back into the tea-room, dragging Charles behind her by the sleeve of his reefer. "Charles would like to kiss you good-bye," she said.
>
> I immediately put down my cup, and said that it was very nice, but was she *sure?*
>
> "Yes," she said, a trifle grimly. She let go Charles's sleeve and gave him a rather vigorous push in my direction. He came forward, his face livid, and gave me a loud, wet smacker just below the right ear. Following this ordeal, he started to make a beeline for the door and a less sentimental way of life, but I caught the half-belt at the back of his reefer, held on to it, and asked him, "What did one wall say to the other wall?"
>
> His face lit up. "Meet you at the corner!" he shrieked, and raced out of the room, probably in hysterics.
>
> Esmé was standing with crossed ankles again. "You're quite sure you won't forget to write that story for me?" she asked. "It doesn't have to be exclusively for me. It can—"
>
> I said there was absolutely no chance that I'd forget. I told her that I'd never written a story *for* anybody, but that it seemed like exactly the right time to get down to it.
>
> She nodded. "Make it extremely squalid and moving," she suggested. "Are you at all acquainted with squalor?"
>
> I said not exactly but that I was getting better acquainted with it, in one form or another, all the time, and that I'd do my best to come up to her specifications. We shook hands.

1

"Isn't it a pity that we didn't meet under less extenuating circumstances?"

I said it was, I said it certainly was.

"Good-bye," Esmé said. "I hope you return from the war with all your faculties intact."

I thanked her, and said a few other words, and then watched her leave the tea-room. She left it slowly, reflectively, testing the ends of her hair for dryness.

The young man put on his robe, closed the lapels tight, and jammed his wet towel into his pocket. He picked up the slimy wet, cumbersome float and put it under his arm. He plodded alone through the soft, hot sand towards the hotel.

On the sub-main floor of the hotel, which the management directed bathers to use, a woman with zinc salve on her nose got into the elevator with the young man.

"I see you're looking at my feet," he said to her when the car was in motion.

"I beg your pardon?" said the woman.

"I said I see you're looking at my feet."

"I beg your pardon. I happened to be looking at the floor," said the woman, and faced the doors of the car.

"If you want to look at my feet, say so," said the young man. "But don't be a God-damned sneak about it."

"Let me out here, please," the woman said quickly to the girl operating the car.

The car doors opened and the woman got out without looking back.

"I have two normal feet and I can't see the slightest God-damned reason why anybody should stare at them," said the young man. "Five, please." He took his room key out of his robe pocket.

He got off at the fifth floor, walked down the hall, and let himself into 507. The room smelled of new calfskin luggage and nail-lacquer remover.

He glanced at the girl lying asleep on one of the twin beds. Then he went over to one of the pieces of luggage, opened it, and from under a pile of shorts and undershirts he took out an Ortgies calibre 7.65 automatic. He released the magazine, looked at it, then reinserted it. He cocked the piece. Then he went over and sat down on the unoccupied twin bed, looked at the girl, aimed the pistol, and fired a bullet through his right temple.

The first extract is from "For Esmé—With Love and Squalor," the second concludes "A Perfect Day for Bananafish." I read them both initially in 1953, when I was not yet twenty-three. Almost sixty years later, I remain charmed by the Esmé story and am still unreconciled to the suicide of Seymour Glass, American saint rushing on to his next reincarnation. To give us Esmé and her little brother, Charles, was an act of the awkward (and awakening) imagination. Seymour, always an irritation, now seems a presumptuous usurpation of fiction for an ill-defined ideological purpose. Keats said that we hate poetry that has a design on us and implicitly praised Shakespeare as the least tendentious of all authors.

D.H. Lawrence's grand admonition was to trust the tale and not the teller. I fiercely trust "For Esmé—With Love and Squalor" but cannot trust Seymour's tale teller. Tendentiousness is not a fault if, like St. Augustine and Sigmund Freud, you have something altogether your own to say. The question thus becomes: What can Salinger give us that Scott Fitzgerald, the American Keats, did not?

GORDON E. SLETHAUG

Seymour: A Clarification

In "A Perfect Day for Bananafish" published in *Nine Stories*, J. D. Salinger has Seymour Glass commit suicide.[1] This seemingly negative and irresponsible action by Seymour has aroused some protest from critics who consider him so unable to cope with reality that he goes insane and shoots himself.[2] Such critics argue that Seymour's reasons and motivations for the suicide are either incomprehensible or of little value to the reader since they are the logic of an escape-oriented madman. This view might indeed be tenable when considering "A Perfect Day for Bananafish" by itself; Seymour's suicide does appear to result merely from his personal instability and a general failure to adjust to the social world. Fortunately, however, Salinger has written "Raise High the Roof Beam, Carpenters," "Seymour—An Introduction," "Franny," "Zooey," and "Hapworth 16, 1924"—all of which deal directly or indirectly with the question of Seymour's personality and his suicide. Except for "Hapworth 16, 1924" which is an extensive letter from the seven-year-old Seymour to his family, these stories deal with Seymour primarily through the comments of his family who revere him highly. The adult Buddy, the brother of Seymour who narrates most of the stories, by his own admission is forty years old, gray-haired, flaccid bottomed, and pot-bellied. Beatrice (Boo Boo) is a middle-class matron who has at least one son mentioned in a short story, "Down at the Dinghy," published in *Nine*

From *Renascence* 23, no. 4 (Summer 1971): 115–28. Copyright © 1971 by the Catholic Renascence Society.

Stories. Walker is a Carthusian monk, and his twin brother, Walt, has been killed in the Second World War. Zooey and Franny, the two youngest of the Glass children, are both actors following the precedent of their parents, Bessie and Les Glass, who have long been involved in vaudeville routines and other forms of show business. All the children, in fact, have appeared in childhood on the radio program, "It's A Wise Child," designed to show how precocious young children can be. And all of the Glass children are precocious, evidencing considerable insight and wisdom. It is safe to assume that there have never been seven such brilliant children in fiction—seven almost surely being a number symbolic of perfection and fulfillment for Salinger.

Salinger deals with Seymour's personality and suicide in the first of the Glass family stories, then explains and vindicates both personality and suicide in the later stories. Although Salinger readily moves back and forth in history, previous to and following Seymour's suicide, he seems to have written the later stories to explain the first; that is, "A Perfect Day for Bananafish" functions as an enigma or a parable clarified by subsequent parables or explanations. Salinger uses this technique frequently. For example, "Franny" is the situation or parable which "Zooey" explains through discussion; "Raise High the Roof Beam, Carpenters" is the parable or situation which "Seymour—An Introduction" explains. Given Salinger's predilection to use the parable and gloss form, he clearly uses "A Perfect Day for Bananafish" in just that fashion.[3]

* * *

From comments in "A Perfect Day for Bananafish" and "Raise High the Roof Beam, Carpenters," the motivation for Seymour's suicide strikes us as most curious. Seymour attempted suicide previously by wrecking his father-in-law's automobile and by slashing his wrists, which acts cause his wife's mother to regard Seymour as insane. The mother-in-law, Mrs. Fedder (as we discover in "Raise High"), definitely wants Seymour locked up or committed entirely to a psychiatrist's care. What Seymour says and does in fact projects the image of an insane person. He calls his wife, Muriel, "Miss Spiritual Tramp of 1948"; he refuses to take off his bathrobe and go swimming; he seems completely abstracted in suggesting that a yellow bathing suit is really blue; he tells a seemingly incomprehensible story about bananafish; and he rankles when a woman in an elevator appears to be looking at his feet. In addition, we have other vague comments from the mother-in-law about Seymour saying strange things to "Granny" concerning her plans for dying and about his doing vaguely horrible things to a window, to an actress friend, to Granny's chair and to some pictures from Bermuda. In "Raise High the Roof Beam, Carpenters," both women make other damning comments about Seymour. Mrs. Fedder considers Seymour a latent homosexual because he fears marriage and because he does not seduce Muriel before the wedding. She considers him a "schizoid personality" because he withdraws from and relates poorly with people and because he'd like to be a dead cat. The Matron of Honour at Seymour's wedding also believes Seymour is schizoid because he says "he's too *happy* to get married." She further notes that Seymour's "somebody that's either never *grown up* or is just an absolute raving maniac of some crazy kind"—"raving maniac" echoing Mrs. Fedder's feeling about Seymour in "A Perfect Day for Bananafish." If the mother-in-law and the Matron were sophisticated enough to attribute psychological tags to his actions, they might call them autistic. That is, the actions seem negative, individually rather than socially oriented.

In "A Perfect Day for Bananafish," Seymour is idiosyncratic in other ways that might relate to the motivation for his suicide. First of all, he is artistically sensitive as indicated by his liking poetry and playing the piano. (Artistic people are traditionally thought to be unstable and unreasonable, and Seymour fits that archetypal pattern.) In one instance, he regards a German author so highly that he suggests to his astonished wife that she learn German in order to read the poems.

Seymour also deviates from social conventions by relating better with little children than with his wife. Consequently, while his wife lies on the bed in the hotelroom, talking with her mother, relating that Seymour will not take off his bathrobe and swim, Seymour is down on the beach taking off his bathrobe and swimming with a little girl named Sybil. He thus caters to the child's preferences more than to his wife's. He has an uncanny ability to fascinate little children like Sybil, knowing what kind of ingenious and slightly childish response they like. For instance, when Sybil complains that Seymour has allowed the three-and-a-half-year-old Sharon Lipschutz to sit on the piano bench with him, he replies:

> "I couldn't push her off, could I?"
> "Yes."
> "Oh, no. No. I couldn't do that," said the young man. "I'll tell you what I did do, though."
> "What?"
> "I pretended she was you."

His response satisfies Sybil and upon his suggestion that they try to catch bananafish in the water, she readily agrees.

The bananafish story Seymour tells also seems idiosyncratic. He tells Sybil that "This is a *perfect* day for bananafish." Then he tells about the fish:

"Their habits are very peculiar, *very* peculiar." He kept push-
ing the float. The water was not quite up to his chest. "They lead
a very tragic life," he said. . . .

"Well, they swim into a hole where there's a lot of bananas.
They're very ordinary-looking fish when they swim *in*. But once
they get in, they behave like pigs. Why, I've known some bananafish to swim into a banana hole and eat as many as seventy-eight
bananas. . . . Naturally after that they're so fat they can't get out
of the hole again. Can't fit through the door."

. . .

"They die."

After the explanation about the bananafish, Sybil confesses to seeing one
with six bananas in its mouth, whereupon Seymour gets out of the water,
walks to his hotel room, and commits suicide. The bananafish story and the
suicide seem closely, if not causally, related.

Because Seymour does appear somewhat insane, because he is a bit idiosyncratic, the reader might well judge his suicide the result of mental instability. That certainly cannot be ruled out. As mentioned in "Zooey," Muriel's
mother believes that if Seymour could just see a psychoanalyst and get his
social behavior straightened out, he would be acceptable. But Zooey suggests
that the psychoanalysts are responsible for the death of Seymour. He says
to his mother, Bessie: "'If you get any more ideas, like last night, of phoning
Philly Byrnes' goddamn psychoanalyst for Franny, just do one thing—that's
all I ask. Just think of what analysis did for Seymour.'" Granted, Zooey simply tries to frighten Bessie out of getting a psychoanalyst for Franny; even
so, Zooey suggests that the psychoanalyst's prying into Seymour's mind, his
attempts to mould Seymour into a normal, well-rounded, fully acceptable
social being, were catastrophic. In "Franny" Franny's boyfriend, Lane, epitomizes the psychological approach when he tells Franny that behind her own
and every religious experience lies a psychological phenomenon: "'I don't
think you leave any margin for the most elementary psy*chology*. I mean I
think all those religious experiences have a very obvious psychological background—you know what I mean.'" As Lane explains it, psychology is man's
attempt to understand the irrational in terms of the rational, to explain the
spiritual in terms of the mental and physical. Given the general obtuseness
of Lane and given Zooey's pejorative references to psychologists, we cannot
accept the theories or practices of psychoanalysis. Zooey, in the book of the
same name, states that only one kind of psychoanalyst could help Franny (and
by extension, Seymour):

"For a psychoanalyst to be any good with Franny at all, he'd have to be a pretty peculiar type. I don't know. He'd have to believe that it was through the grace of God that he'd been inspired to study psychoanalysis in the first place. He'd have to believe that it was through the grace of God that he wasn't run over by a goddamn truck before he ever even got his license to practice. He'd have to believe that it's through the grace of God that he has the native intelligence to be able to help his goddamn patients at *all*. I don't know any *good* analysts who think along those lines. But that's the only kind of psychoanalyst who might be able to do Franny any good at all. If she got somebody terribly Freudian, or terribly eclectic, or just terribly run-of-the-mill—somebody who didn't even have any crazy, mysterious *gra*titude for his insight and intelligence—she'd come out of analysis in even worse shape than Seymour did."

Zooey's comments about psychoanalysts needing the "grace of God" to deal with Franny indicates that Mrs. Fedder has incorrectly appraised Seymour's illness and that the nature of both Seymour's malady and Franny's is an intense kind of grace, of spirituality. And before returning to "A Perfect Day for Bananafish," we must fully investigate this "insanity," this kind of illogical, mystical spirituality and the accompanying qualities of acute sense perceptions, love, and poetic and divine inspiration that characterize Seymour.

* * *

Seymour's insanity is really akin to what in "Seymour—An Introduction" Buddy calls "a madness of the heart." In fact, Buddy refers to Seymour as "a *mukta*, a ringding enlightened man, a God-knower." The same narrator further states: "The hallmark, then, of the advanced religious, nonsectarian or any other (and I graciously include in the definition of an 'advanced religious,' odious though the phrase is, all Christians on the great Vivekananda's terms; i.e., 'See Christ, then you are a Christian; all else is talk')—the hallmark most commonly identifying this person is that he very frequently behaves like a fool, even an imbecile." Such spiritual intensity characterizes all of Salinger's insane—Seymour, Franny, and Buddy Glass as well as Holden Caulfield.

Because insanity is so closely linked with spiritual enlightenment and also poetic inspiration and artistry, it is necessary that we look carefully at the nature of this divine inspiration. Perhaps we must logically begin with the ethnic background of the Glass children. As Buddy emphasizes on several occasions, they are of mixed Jewish and Irish extraction. He particularly notes that both the Irish and Jewish predecessors were involved in song-and-dance vaudeville routines or circus equivalents. Hence, Salinger uses the typical contemporary denotation of the Jewish and Irish as great natural clowns or actors. But Buddy also mentions Seymour's Semitic blood in relation to his writing poetry. The allusion suggests that Seymour's predilection for mysticism may result from the Jewish-Irish background; that is, these two ethnic groups are commonly viewed as the repositories for the poetry and prophesy of the Judaic-Christian tradition. Both cultures are steeped in religious mysticism. Thus the ethnic background helps to explain the natural affinity for acting within the family and also the affinity for mystical religious insights.

Seymour's mystically spiritual insight negates reason and logic. The most precise expression of the necessity and value of irrationality for religious insight comes from "Teddy," an earlier story by Salinger in *Nine Stories* (which, from comments in "Seymour—An Introduction," Buddy appears to have written). Teddy, in trying to explain how he achieved a mystical experience, how he "saw that everything was God," answers: "'You asked me how I get out of the finite dimensions when I feel like it. I certainly don't use logic when I do it. Logic's the first thing you have to get rid of.'" In another place Teddy says in reference to Eden: "'You know what was in that apple? Logic. Logic and intellectual stuff. That was all that was in it.'" In his letter, "Hapworth 16, 1924," written to his family when he was seven years old, Seymour reflects Teddy's sentiment. He states that one can enter into the mind and knowledge of God only by the suspension of logic: "I will assume temporarily that these instructions [of God] will prove potent, effective, encouraging, and quite intensive, provided I hold my mind quite still and empty. . . ." To hold the mind "still and empty" is to dispel all rational thoughts and logical arguments. The person who tries to make religion a rational and practical concern is regarded as rather stupid by Zooey who satirizes Dr. Homer Vincent Claude Pierson, Jr., the author of a book called "God Is My Hobby"—surely a satiric barb directed against the religious pragmatist, Norman Vincent Peale. One of the basically illogical, impractical, un-Peale-like tenets of the Glass children is a belief in the transmigration of the soul from lower to higher states of existence.[4] Each stage—which Seymour calls an "appearance"—is an act in the great evolving drama of human life as controlled by God. Buddy and Seymour recall several of their own previous stages of existence as well as of others. Seymour knows, for example, that an acquaintance, Mr. Happy, mentioned in "Hapworth 16, 1924," "made ropes in his previous appearance, but not very well. . . . He was executed for making a defective rope, resulting in the deaths of some influential climbers. . . ." Seymour talks about the responsibilities of his present appearance, believing that he brings his "creative genius" from a previous appearance and that he must do considerable "good in this appearance." When man has fulfilled such obligations in an appearance, then he must pass on to another. As Seymour writes to Bessie and Les: "However, when we have fulfilled our opportunities and obligations, dear Bessie and Les, I give you my word that we will depart in good conscience and humor for a change, which we have never entirely done in the past." He further knows as a seven year old that he will live only about thirty years in this appearance. Most important to an understanding of Salinger's fiction is this concept that Seymour, by thinking in terms of appearances, of a limited time in this appearance, and of his obligations to fulfill the plan of God, does not act stupidly or insanely but very wisely. The wisdom is not the wisdom of Western logic that demands the rejection of the idea of transmigration of the soul, but the wisdom of the Glass's intuition based upon the Oriental religions and the Romantic tradition.[5]

In addition to his reliance on intuition, Seymour as a seven year old believes that the alternative to wrongheaded logic is "to fall back on the flimsy information offered in excellent faith by our eyes, hands, ears, and simple, heart-rending brains." The alternative choice involves a reliance upon sense perception and emotion-guided thoughts. (Salinger quite surely uses "heart-rending brains" to indicate that logic must be controlled by the emotions of the heart.) In keeping with Seymour's comment, Salinger's characters with religious insight frequently emphasize what they see, hear, or touch. Buddy notes in "Seymour—An Introduction" that Seymour, for instance, "once said, on the air, when he was eleven, that the thing he loved best in the Bible was the word WATCH!" The young Seymour in "Hapworth 16, 1924" mentions "seeing" and says in a moment of joy: "Jesus, life has its share of honorable thrills if one but keeps one's eyes open!" As a corollary to Seymour's statement, Bessie is told by her youngest son in "Zooey" that the book called *The Pilgrim Continues His Way* provides an explanation of "keeping one's eyes open," of insight: " . . . in Eastern terms, there are seven subtle centers in the body, called *chakras*, and the one most closely connected with the heart is called *anahata*, which is supposed to be sensitive and powerful as hell, and when it's activated, it, in turn, activates another of these centers, between the eyebrows, called *ajna*—it's the pineal gland, really, or, rather, an aura around the pineal gland—and then, bingo, there's an opening of what mystics call the 'third eye.'" Zooey also states that the purpose of the book is "to wake everybody up" to their spiritual needs. To see is to look carefully and deeply at the surrounding world, so as to perceive its spiritual implication. One who sees truly, then, is a seer; and the real seers are the innocents, fools, the poets and painters—those individuals frequently cited as seers by the Transcendentalists, Thoreau and

Emerson, to whom Salinger owes a great literary debt.[6] As Buddy queries in "Seymour—An Introduction": "Isn't the true poet or painter a seer? Isn't he, actually, the only seer we have on earth?" He also states that "the true artist-seer [is] . . . the heavenly fool who can and does produce beauty. . . ." The wise man, then, must look for "beauty," that quality of spiritual being that pervades every single object. (It should be noted that "beautiful" is an extremely important word for Salinger. In "Hapworth 16, 1924," for instance, Seymour speaks of beautiful things as those particular unrelated phenomena which, when regarded correctly, indicate to the viewer God's working in man's life and even possibly indicate the order of the universe: "I find it magnificent how beautiful, loose ends find each other in the world if one only waits with decent patience, resilience, and quite blind strength.") Seymour surely is this wise man who perceives beauty, the true spiritual beauty, as Buddy's description of his eyes indicates in "Seymour—An Introduction": "In reality, there was something like a here-again, gone-again, super-gossamer cast over his eyes—except that it wasn't a cast at all, and *that* was where I ran into trouble." His eyes symbolize his poetic, divine insight.

As with the quality of seeing, the quality of hearing must be acute enough to sense spiritual implications. And as with his eyes, Seymour's ears are extraordinary. According to Buddy in "Seymour—An Introduction," Seymour had "the ears of an old cabalist or an old Buddha." The allusion to cabalist suggests the perceiving of occult truths and the allusion to Buddha the perceiving of divine truths. Buddy further perceives that Seymour particularly likes Oriental poetry and frequently writes haiku himself because it is "fine for the ear." The very sound of poetry, or perhaps the very sound of truth as it is communicated through poetry, appeals to Seymour. Both ear and eye, then, must be employed in the search and discovery of spiritual absolutes. To be a prophetic "seer" one must also be able to hear the divine sounds that permeate the universe. In one of Salinger's early stories, "The Varioni Brothers," published in *The Saturday Evening Post*, Sonny Varioni discovers the extraordinary effect of reading his brother Joe's unpublished novel: he hears "music" for the first time in his life.[7] The story suggests that to "hear music" is to understand the divine, to perceive the delicately and divinely ordered operations of life—a contemporary approximation of the Pythagorean concept of hearing the harmony of the spheres.

As with seeing and hearing, so with breathing. In the Glass stories Salinger uses a good deal of imagery pertaining to breathing and smelling. Among the most important of such images is smoking. Nearly all of Salinger's important heroes smoke, among them Buddy, Franny, Zooey, and Seymour Glass and Holden Caulfield. All of these characters are addicted to smoking—but perhaps for a spiritual reason. That is, to smoke in Salinger's novels is often to think deeply and clearly and spiritually. The act of inhaling indicates a meditative process, a process whereby one develops insight in a situation where insight and wisdom come none too easily. Such is the purport of the narrator's comment in "Zooey" concerning Zooey's smoking a cigar when trying to talk to Franny about her spiritual quest: "He picked up his cigar from the lip of the copper ashtray where he had placed it. It was now only about two inches in length but was still burning. He took a deep drag on it, as if it were a kind of respirator in an otherwise oxygenless world." Young Seymour states yet another reason for smoking: the recognition of an absolute force. He writes to his father, Les, in "Hapworth 16, 1924": "Les, . . . I know you toy honorably with disbelief in God or Providence, or which ever word you find less maddening or embarrassing, but I give you my word of honor, on this sultry, memorable day of my life, that one cannot even light a casual cigarette unless the artistic permission of the universe is freely given!" For Seymour, then, the simple and very minor incident of smoking, evidently the epitome of breathing, reflects the absolute sovereignty and perfection of God—precisely his comment about all acts of breathing, seeing, and hearing.

Another of the senses important to Seymour is touch. Critics have been overly quick to assume, as does Baumbach, that Salinger's heroes and indeed Salinger himself manifest latent homosexuality, particularly with reference to Antolini touching Holden's hair.[8] But what appears to be homosexuality is simply human beings wanting to touch others, to feel a kind of essential contact. In his diary, as described in "Raise High the Roof Beam, Carpenters," Seymour writes, "'If or when I do start going to an analyst, I hope to God he has the foresight to let a dermatologist sit in on consultation. A hand specialist. I have scars on my hands from touching certain people. . . . Certain heads, certain colors and textures of human hair leave permanent marks on me. Other things, too. Charlotte once ran away from me, outside the studio, and I grabbed her dress to stop her, to keep her near me. . . . I still have a lemon-yellow mark on the palm of my right hand.'" The Charlotte he refers to is the same actress that Mrs. Fedder mentions his hurting. He had not intended to hurt her, just to hold her. In "Seymour—An Introduction," Buddy calls Seymour's sensitive hands "very fine," even "beautiful," thereby indicating their spiritual nature. When Buddy mentions the fineness of his brother's hands, he admits that by raising the issue some readers might think Buddy himself homosexual: "To what extent, I wonder, may one be allowed to admire one's brother's hands without raising a few modern eyebrows? In my youth, Father William, my heterosexuality (discounting a few, shall I say, not always quite voluntary slow periods) was often rather common gossip in some of my old Study Groups." Quite clearly, Buddy discounts the idea that the beauty and sensitivity of hands or his comments on them have anything at all to do with homosexuality. (And by raising the issue of the hands, Buddy clarifies a few enigmatic problems in the Glass stories: one, of the silent old man putting his hand into Buddy's after Seymour's momentarily abortive wedding and two, of Franny's always touching her forehead. In the first, the old man and Buddy, without words of any sort, feel a human relationship. In the second, by Franny's touching her forehead, the seat of her thinking powers, she indicates her relationship with the infinite, a spiritual touching.) As Buddy recollects in "Seymour—An Introduction," another important instance of touch is Seymour's hair jumping to Buddy's chair when as youths, they had hair cuts. That Seymour's hair should quite cover Buddy indicates the amazing way in which Seymour would reach out to embrace his fellow human beings. As a Whitmanesque corollary to the idea of people touching one another, the seven-year-old Seymour delightedly notes in his letter that "everybody seated in the library has a gall bladder and various other, touching organs under their skin." The organs touching one another suggests that "ninety-eight per cent of . . . life, thank God, has nothing to do with the dubious pursuit of knowledge." In other words, life mainly concerns man's relation to other human beings and to God, not the accumulation of knowledge.

The combined qualities of seeing, hearing, breathing, and touching indicate the basic means for coming to terms with life: to look carefully and deliberately at the surrounding environment, to intuit deeply the nature of God permeating and influencing all life, and to feel affectionately for all human and non-human creatures—the very means advocated by the American Transcendentalists. The concept is one of a basic reverence for and delight in man's spiritual and material (earth-bound) life.

*   *   *

Delight in life is one of Seymour's more remarkable characteristics. As young Seymour states in "Hapworth 16, 1924," every action he undertakes should be marked by "affection or inspiration"—the twin qualities of existence. He further notes that his "personal instability and too much emotion will ever be plainly marked in every stroke of the pen, quite unfortunately." The Glass family stories abound with references to both the qualities of affection and inspiration—and both relate to Seymour's being a poet. As a youth, Seymour states: "If the person or the person's contributions have not roused his love and unexplainable happiness or eternal warmth, that person must be ruthlessly severed from the list [of people to be consulted!" Every action must be imbued with love, happiness and eternal warmth. Because Seymour was so loving and happy upon being married, he did not want his happiness dulled by an insensitive audience watching the ceremony. But in another instance, Seymour indicates that the ultimate in love, happiness, and warmth, is to perform for and in spite of the gross audience. For that reason, in "Zooey" he tells his youngest brother to shine his shoes for the "Fat Lady" in the audience of the children's radio program "It's a Wise Child" and for that reason, he feels deep affection for Mrs. Overman in "Hapworth 16, 1924." An audience of a fat lady or a librarian who is a fussy old spinster represents a most gross, unappreciative audience, one extremely difficult to perform for excellently. Seymour indicates that a truly divine gesture is to love that gross audience so incapable of returning one's love. By performing for a gross audience, as well as a good one, Seymour learns the art of self-perfection. Young Seymour explains in "Hapworth 16, 1924" that he is "utterly convinced that if A's hat blows off while he is sauntering down the street, it is the charming duty of B to pick it up and hand it to A without examining A's face or combing it for gratitude! My God, let me achieve missing my beloved family without yearning that they quite miss me in return!" Such is the substance of the Christian concept of *agape*, to love without expecting returned love, to love that which is the most unloving. To achieve love, happiness, and eternal warmth, then, is to fulfill the criteria of *agape*. Although Salinger attributes the purity of love mainly to children, Seymour is one of the rare, believable individuals in literature who can love in such a pure manner without seeming didactic or overly sentimental. (He is, of course, sentimental—but not overly so. For instance, in "Raise High the Roof Beam, Carpenters," he cries a good deal from sheer happiness; and in "Hapworth 16, 1924," he constantly refers to the Glass family members as "Sweetheart" and to animals as "sweet"—both "sweet" and "sweetheart" evidently in the Medieval sense of blessed.) Seymour manifests a childlike love and acceptance of others. And associated with Seymour are two symbols of innocence, the first is the symbol of a child's foot and the second, the color blue. Seymour often emphasizes the appearance of feet. As a youngster, he writes to his family: "You know yourselves what an unexpected bonus it is to run into a fully grown adult with splendid or even quite presentable toes in the last analysis; usually, disastrous things happen to the toes after they leave a darling child's body. . . ." The appearance of childlike feet thus seems an outward symbol of some kind of inner grace which only children and poets have. The color blue functions as a related symbol indicative of innocence and love. In Salinger's fiction, the innocents who give spiritual succor to adults most often wear blue clothing or have blue eyes. Holden's sister, Phoebe, wears blue pajamas and a blue coat for instance. Salinger's adults who have blue eyes or wear blue, such as Bessie and Franny, may not always give spiritual succor, but they evidence intense love—a quality closely related to innocence.

Besides emphasizing love, happiness, and eternal warmth—the qualities that make possible kindness and compassion for others—Seymour finds inspiration a great value for human beings. He remarks in "Hapworth 16, 1924": "Close on the heels of kindness, originality is one of the most thrilling things in the world, also the most rare!" The originality that Seymour seeks particularly resides in asocial fools, the seers and the poets mentioned above. Since this originality resides in the poetic sort of person, the originality must also be present in poetry. According to Buddy in "Seymour—An Introduction," the kind of poetry that conveys the most profound, original thoughts are Seymour's and his poetic models, the Chinese and Japanese verse, which "Seymour wrote and talked . . . thirty one years. . . ." Buddy says of the Oriental poetry: "At their most effective, I believe, Chinese and Japanese classical verses are intelligible utterances that please or enlighten or enlarge the invited eavesdropper to within an inch of his life." Poetry has as its everyday function the enlightening of man to a more original perception of truth. The truth need not be a vision of the total plan of the universe, but simply an insight into one small, simple, and beautiful daily occurrence ("small," "simple," and "beautiful" being loaded adjectives for Salinger). Seymour argues in "Raise High the Roof Beam, Carpenters," that the poetry a man writes must present an image of "the main current of poetry that flows through things, all things." Seymour's poems do show the poetry that flows through things and have so much originality and spiritual impact that they "burn" Buddy. Buddy further notes that Seymour is so original as to be one of the "three or four *very* nearly nonexpendable poets."

Poetry has as its function, then, not just the technical brilliance of fine artistry but the revelation of wisdom through images; it leads the reader to a state of wisdom—like the professed rhetorical purpose of euphuistic poetry in the Renaissance. Franny distinguishes between "real" poets who are wise and lead the reader to wisdom and those who are simply technically brilliant. For a writer-poet to be brilliant, to accumulate data and facts to impress an audience in a classroom or cocktail party is not using knowledge in a correct way. Franny's famous anti-academic comment in "Zooey" emphasizes "that college was just one more *dopey, inane* place in the world dedicated to piling up treasure on earth and everything. I mean treasure is *trea*sure, for heaven's sake. What's the difference whether the treasure is money, or property, or even *cul*ture, or even just plain knowledge? . . . knowledge *should* lead to *wisdom*, and . . . if it *doesn't*, it's just a disgusting waste of time!" In response to Franny's outburst, Zooey distinguishes between different uses of knowledge, degrees of wisdom. He finds that, as a representative individual, he either turns "into a goddamn *seer* or a human hatpin." That is, he can perceive ultimate reality as a seer or he can expend his energy satirizing what he finds around him.

He recommends the "seer" above the "hatpin." To be a good poet is to live as a wise seer and communicate that wisdom in some way to someone else, perhaps not even through a poem. Young Seymour, in fact, says in his letter from camp that "It is my absolute opinion that the only poem of personal, haunting interest to me that I have written so far this summer is one I have not written at all." The comment first strikes the reader as absurd: how can one have written a poem that he has not written? But what Seymour means is approximate to Thoreau's artistically questionable lines of poetry from *A Week On The Concord And Merrimack Rivers*:

My life has been the poem I would have writ,
But I could not both live and utter it.[9]

In "Raise High the Roof Beam, Carpenters," Buddy clarifies Seymour's position by admitting: "If he never wrote a line of poetry, he could still flash what he had at you with the back of his ear if he wanted to." Seymour, then, values life as a poem. And the only potentially perfect poem is one's own life. For that reason, Seymour must live and die in a particularly exemplary way.

* * *

Regarding the individual's life, particularly Seymour's, as exemplary makes sense of some of his actions and comments in "A Perfect Day for Bananafish" and the other fiction. If his life is exemplary, and if exemplary means to act in the most divine way possible, then Seymour must fulfill the dictates given by God. A primary dictate is to act purely. Since Seymour knows that he inclines toward sensuality over spirituality, he feels he must understand and accept the quality of sensuality, and then triumph over it. In "Hapworth 16, 1924," he calls this "karmic responsibility; one meets it, one conquers it, or if one does not conquer it, one enters into honorable contest with it, seeking and giving no quarter." As a seven year old, he intensely lusts after some of the mature women at Camp Hapworth; but by the time he goes with Muriel, Mrs. Fedder thinks him a homosexual because he does not make love to Muriel before marriage. Obviously Seymour does, to some extent, conquer that ruling passion; he brings it into a proper focus and relationship with the spiritual.

Because Seymour believes in living purely, he regards all existence in an intensely spiritual manner. When he or someone else fails to live purely, he humorously derides the impure act. Thus in "A Perfect Day for Bananafish," the initial parable which we have been explaining by means of the later novellas, he calls Muriel "Miss Spiritual Tramp of 1945" and he attempts to have her read some inspired German poetry to increase her spiritual perception. But Muriel is too materialistic, too concerned with spending money to make herself sexy, too concerned with a good room in a prestigious hotel, in short too concerned with herself. She is a spiritual tramp and refuses to attempt a more poetic way of life. Because she is spiritually decadent, Seymour sometimes can not relate to her.

But when someone lives purely, Seymour enjoys a unique relationship with that person. He particularly likes to associate with the innocents, the spiritual children, and likes to dwell upon images of innocence. For such a reason, he makes friends with the little girl Sybil. With Sybil he associates innocence as indicated by his calling her yellow bathing suit blue and by his kissing the arch of her youthful foot. (As mentioned above he is sensitive about a person's feet. It seems that his own feet must have been particularly youthful because the lady in the elevator looked at them intensely.) He relates easily to her, bantering in a playfully illogical manner and vacillating between fact and fantasy while talking about Whirly Wood, Connecticut, about Little Black Sambo and the six tigers, and about Sharon Lipschutz, the friend of Seymour and Sybil. In this oddly humorous conversation, some of Seymour's basic values appear. He reveres the existence of all life, and he expects that both animals and human beings be treated compassionately and lovingly. Even if human beings are so egocentric and spiritually corrupt as his wife Muriel, he expects that they be treated with the reverence due all life. It is also through his conversation with Sybil that he becomes aware of the necessity of terminating his life. Her ancient Doric name means "the will of God" and suggests the power of divination and prophetic utterance; she serves as the prophetess of his death. After Seymour tells Sybil that parable of the bananafish, she supposedly sees one fish with six bananas in its mouth. If this parable has a specific interpretation, it suggests that each man is a bananafish partaking and even gorging himself on life. He must live life to its fullest, and after he has gorged himself to the extreme, he must die. By Sybil's stating that she sees the fish, she reminds Seymour that his time has elapsed, and he must not dally in this life but go to another. One of the supreme tests in life is to fulfill the ordinance of Fate concerning one's life and death. That is, if Fate decrees that one should continue an acting career or die at thirty-one, then an individual should not object. In "Hapworth 16, 1924," Seymour told Bessie as much about her life: if you forsake a remarkable career at the chipper age of 28, no matter how many illustrious years you already have under your belt, you will be tampering with fate out of season. In season, to be sure, fate can be dealt stunning blows, but out of season, regrettably, mistakes are quite usual and costly." In that same letter, he says of himself: "My time is too limited, quite to my sadness and amusement." Because Seymour understands that he must die at an early age, he has little time to accomplish his obligations; he must act speedily. And since he always foresaw the time of his own death, he acts in accordance with the divine dictate. In short, his several attempts at suicide indicate that this "appearance" is finished, this incarnation is done and he must hasten along to another incarnation: he must not fight God. So Seymour's suicide is the utmost in his commitment to God; he acts according to God's wishes. It has little or nothing to do with inability to live in this world; it has nothing to do with escapism; it has everything to do with acceptance of spiritual responsibility. Seymour's insanity and ensuing suicide, then, should not elicit an unfavourable response from the readers. Seymour is not negative and irresponsible; within the Glass world created by Salinger, Seymour's particular sort of spiritual insight and suicide form the most dedicated commitment to a divinely ordained pattern of life.

Notes

1. Boston, 1953. Other editions of Salinger's major works which are cited in this essay include: *Raise High the Roof Beam, Carpenters and Seymour An Introduction* (Boston, 1959); *Franny and Zooey* (Boston, 1955); and "Hapworth 16, 1924," *The New Yorker*, 41, pt. 3 (June 19, 1965), 32–113.

2. Among the critics who believe that Seymour cannot cope with reality are Frederick L. Gwynn and Joseph L. Blotner, *The Fiction of J. D. Salinger* (Pittsburgh, 1960), pp. 19–21. They believe that Seymour simply and pathetically kills himself because Muriel fails to show him love. William Wiegand, "The Cures for Banana Fever," *Salinger: A Critical and Personal Portrait*, ed. Henry Anatole Grunwald (New York, 1962), p. 125, argues that Seymour is the victim of a bourgeois matriarchy. Wiegand and James E. Miller, Jr., *J. D. Salinger* (Minneapolis, 1965), pp. 28–29, think that Seymour dies because he is glutted with physical sensations. Warren French, *J. D. Salinger* (New York, 1963), p. 84, finds that Seymour dies because he has an "insatiable appetite, for attention." In contrast to the above critics, Kenneth Hamilton, *J. D. Salinger* (Grand Rapids, Michigan, 1967), p. 30, defends Seymour's suicide as an act of self-sacrifice designed to liberate Muriel from an unhappy marriage. Hamilton almost makes Seymour out to be a Christ figure.

3. Janus E. Miller, Jr., *J. D. Salinger*, p. 27, and Wiegand, "The Cures for Banana Fever," p. 132, both note that the "Bananafish" story is explained to some extent by the later Glass stories. Critics by no means, however, agree about whether to, or how to, interpret the short story in relation to the novellas. I, for one, am singularly convinced that the later stories do not change the image of Seymour; rather they enlarge his personality and enlighten the reader as to his total view of life.

4. Although I can find no firm support in any of Seymour's or Buddy's statements, I believe that the acting careers of the Glass family may tie in with the doctrine of the transmigration of the soul. Even as an actor performs scene after act after drama, so man in Salinger's cosmos lives year after life after successive lives fulfilling the great plan of the universe.

5. By pointing toward Salinger's use of Oriental religions, I do not commit myself to the supposition that Salinger has embraced some form of Eastern religion, be it Buddhism, Hinduism or Taoism. The persistent religious trend within his writing seems much more eclectic, drawing from both Oriental religion and Christianity.

6. As Grunwald notes in his introduction to *Salinger*, Salinger's style and content most frequently have been compared to F. Scott Fitzgerald's, Ring Lardner's, and Mark Twain's. I find, however, that the most persuasive influence and literary credit is due the Romantics culminating with the Transcendentalists, Thoreau and Emerson. Granted the style is not very Transcendental, but the content surely is very much within that American tradition as I hope to demonstrate in a following article. One who sees Salinger within this tradition is Carl F. Strauch, "Salinger: The Romantic Background," *WSCL*, IV (Winter 1963), 31–40.

7. CCXVI (July 17, 1943), pp. 12–13, 76–77.

8. Jonathan Baumbach, "The Saint As A Young Man: A Reappraisal of *The Catcher In The Rye*," *MLQ*, XXV (December 1964), 463.

9. *The Writings of Henry David Thoreau*, Walden Edition, 20 vols. (Boston, 1906), I, 365.

GARY LANE

Seymour's Suicide Again: A New Reading of J. D. Salinger's "A Perfect Day for Bananafish"

The suicide of Seymour Glass in "A Perfect Day for Bananafish" has troubled readers and critics alike; despite the considerable attention paid it, its meaning has remained uncomfortably uncertain. Seymour, it is sometimes suggested, "unable to tolerate the everyday sensations of his tiresome, postwar life," has simply "lost his mind."[1] This theory, however, emphasizes unduly the Seymour we hear about from other characters—the kind and gentle man we actually meet on the beach seems eccentric but eminently sane—and fails to explain convincingly, among other things, the clearly allegorical tale of the bananafish. Other critics feel that Seymour, for all his obvious intelligence, remains a child, that he "does many things—intentionally or unintentionally—to disrupt others' composure" and to gain thereby their attention. "He has tried in increasingly conspicuous ways to upset [Muriel, and] . . . finally, as with the child so desperate for the desired attention that it will risk injury, there remains but one thing he can do—he can shoot himself. Then she will have to pay attention; then her iron composure will be disrupted. She will cry and run hysterically about the hotel room—or so he hopes."[2] Again, though, Muriel is given too much credit; surely the psychotic exhibitionist posited here would spend his vacation at the hotel bar, not on the beach by himself. Closest to the truth, still others suggest, is a more complex position: Seymour's

From *Studies in Short Fiction* 10, no. 1 (Winter 1973): 27–33. Copyright © 1972 by Newberry College.

suicide is not "merely a rejection of this world of crass superficiality, but it is also—and more significantly—a rejection of the mystical life itself."[3] This explanation, however, derives largely from hints in Salinger's later work—its proponents offer little evidence from "Bananafish" to support it—and thereby leads us somewhat astray.[4] We will do better, I think, closer to home. Indeed, there is within the story an important though oblique reference, which, tracked down, may tell us a good deal about Seymour Glass, and in the process help show "Bananafish" to be tighter and more careful than has been supposed.

The reference occurs during the story's opening scene. Muriel, on the telephone with her mother, inquires suddenly about "that book he sent me from Germany . . . those German poems."[5] The book is on Seymour's mind: "he *asked* me about it, when we were driving down. He wanted to know if I'd read it" (p. 7). And, since poetry matters to Seymour—we will note later how telling is his wry allusion to "The Waste Land"—he must feel very close to it, for he considers its author "the *only great poet of the century*" (pp. 7–8). I submit that the poems in question are Rilke's *Duino Elegies*.[6] These last and greatest poems of Rilke, though diverse and difficult, are informed by a basic thematic lamentation over the insufficiency of man and pervaded by a symbolic Angel, the reminder, in his transcendence of human limitation, at once of man's aspiration and necessary failure. The poems are thus reflections about precisely the problems that, as we shall see, oppress Seymour. Indeed, several passages from the *Elegies* correspond so exactly to situations in "Bananafish" that, corroborating other evidence, they furnish a kind of explicative gloss to the story.

We first meet Seymour through the dramatically subjective observations of his wife and mother-in-law. The story begins by introducing us to Muriel, and, significantly, we learn at once that she has been reading an article entitled "Sex Is Fun—or Hell" (p. 3). Far from indicating, however, some sexual problem of Seymour's, this fact gives us an introductory perspective on his wife.[7] As the telephone dialogue unfolds her character, our initial indication is reinforced and amplified; we come to see that, for all her *chic* and poise, Muriel is basically simple—and basically corrupt. She possesses the undisciplined mind of a child, equating things of unequal importance, skipping indiscriminately among conversational topics, and perhaps even expecting to learn something about sex from the knowing writers of women's magazines. Further, she is bored with her mother and her life, baffled but bored with her husband, and complacently, simple-mindedly unconcerned with everyone. It is through this rather dense filter that our first light on Seymour passes, and we must allow for a certain amount of refraction when we hear it implied that Seymour is confusing, crude, and dangerously near the brink of mental unbalance. Of greater importance are the book he has sent Muriel and the fact that he will not remove his bathrobe on the beach, and, as will become clear, the former is a key to the latter.

When Muriel's phone call is finished, the scene abruptly shifts, and the import of the change, from hotel room and gossip of Seymour to the beach and the man himself, is heralded at once: here, as the unconsciously oracular Sybil unconsciously announces, we will find the real "see more glass" (p. 14). The man on the beach is kind and brilliant, ironic and questioning, but quite sane. His encounter with the child, during which the decision for suicide is made final, calls to mind first this passage from Rilke's *Fourth Elegy*:

> Wer zeigt ein Kind, so wie es steht? Wer stellt
> es ins Gestirn und gibt das Mass des Abstands
> ihm in die Hand? Wer macht den Kindertod
> aus grauem Brot, das hart wird,—oder lässt
> ihn drin im runden Mund so wie den Gröps
> von einem schönen Apfel?. . . . Mörder sind
> leicht einzusehen. Aber dies: den Tod,
> den ganzen Tod, noch vor dem Leben so
> sanft zu enthalten und nicht bös zu sein,
> ist unbeschreiblich.

> Who'll show a child just as it is? Who'll place it
> within its constellation, with the measure
> of distance in its hand? Who make its death
> from grey bread, that grows hard,—or leave it there,
> within the round mouth, like the choking core
> of a sweet apple?. . . . Minds of murderers
> are easily divined. But this, though: death,
> the whole of death,—even before life's begun,
> to hold it all so gently, and be good:
> this is beyond description![8]

Seymour, in the story, experiences the same poignant perception of the nearness to death, and hence infinity, that the child's imaginative and self-supporting world attains. To see Sybil in her innocence is to see the incomprehensible goodness of the child, who carelessly allows death to live beside it. Yet even in this goodness, which Seymour loves for its simplicity, there are suggestions of imperfection: on the one hand, it is easily corrupted; on the other, it exists unaware of complexities.

For Sybil, after all, is no Rilkean Angel; the clearer our—and Seymour's—perspective on her, the more visibly does the tarnish on her innocence spread like the sun-tan oil down "the delicate, winglike blades of her back" (pp. 14–15). Jealous and possessive, she instructs Seymour, should Sharon Lipschutz again sit by him at the piano, to "Next time, push her off" (p. 19). "Ah, Sharon Lipschutz," he replies, "How that name comes up. Mixing memory and desire" (p. 10). Like the polymorphous narrator of *The Waste Land*, Seymour looks longingly back to a time that can no more exist, a time before he understood that Sharons, "never mean or unkind" (p. 22), turn soon into Sybils, who "poke . . . little dog[s] with balloon sticks" (p. 22), and that Sybils, at least spontaneous and honest, grow thence to Muriels.[9] Besides, Sybil's bathing suit is *yellow* and she *lives* in Whirly Wood, Connecticut. Seymour's apparently irrational statements about these things are his ironic recognition that the child's simple, sure mind, if more comfortable than his own, is no more infinite, no more transcendent; it is the very failure to understand that keeps the child close to death. The remarks are the *Kläge* of the *Elegies*, laments for man's mortality, for Seymour, like Rilke, in knowing much becomes inextricably entangled in the divine web that the limited mortal must try to spin.

The symbol of this aspiring but defeating mortality, the constant reminder that

> Ja, die Frühlinge brauchten dich wohl. Es muteten manche
> Sterne dir zu, dass du sie spürtest. Es hob
> sich eine Woge heran im Vergangenen, oder
> da du vorüberkamst am geöffneten Fenster,
> gab eine Geige sich hin. Das alles war Auftrag.
> Aber bewältigtest du's? Warst du nicht immer
> noch von Erwartung zerstreut, als kündigte alles
> eine Geliebte dir an?

> Yes, the springs had need of you. Many a star
> was waiting for you to espy it. Many a wave
> would rise on the past towards you; or, else, perhaps,
> as you went by an open window, a violin
> would be giving itself to someone. All this was a trust.
> But were you equal to it? Were you not always
> distracted by expectation, as though all this
> were announcing someone to love?[10]

is for Seymour his tattoo, his body. And, though he explains to Muriel that he "doesn't want a lot of fools looking at his tattoo" (p. 14), it is a lonely part of beach he is on, and, as he says to Sybil, "What a fool I am" (p. 17)! It is Seymour himself who does not wish to confront the symbol of what his mind cannot surmount. When at last he removes the robe, faces squarely the insoluble problem of himself as man, Seymour decides that fully realized love is not to be found in life. He has loved Sybil for her bright, child's being, but, realizing her inadequacies, seen in her the seedling of a future Muriel. The remaining way is that which Rilke calls the "less illuminated" side of life, death. The bananafish story is Seymour's parable of his defeat in life and decision for death: Seymour, coming into the world with a rare capacity for love, takes too much aspiration to it, becomes trapped by man's imperfect mortality, and must die.

We can see now why Salinger devised the careful and ominous structural parallel between the second scene and the first. In both we begin with a girl and her mother—each, appearances notwithstanding, basically uninterested in the other—who talk, without communicating or understanding, about Seymour; in both we end with a severed connection and a girl, unregretful and alone. We see clearly the differences between the implied psychotic of scene one and the actual man on the beach, but the structure warns us not to overlook the similarities of the women involved. For when we understand those similarities—and recognize that they represent not Holden Caulfield's adolescent and self-excluding conception of a world of phonies, but the sad and adult realization that all humanity, Seymour self-consciously included, is limited and corruptible—we can see the *cul de sac* from which Seymour would escape.

Salinger emphasizes the universality of this condition with his choice of names. Seymour Glass is the Emersonian poet, the man who "turns the world to glass" and, like Seymour in Florida, "must pass for a fool and a churl for a long season";[11] he is the sensitive barometer of the weather of human possibility, and the conditions he reacts against are irreversible. Perhaps he is as well Wallace Stevens' "impossible possible philosopher's man,"

The man who has had the time to think enough,
The central man, the human globe, responsive
As a mirror with a voice, the man of glass,
Who in a million diamonds sums us up.[12]

Sybil, bright with innocence but already tarnishing, symbolizes for Seymour the human condition: like the sibyls of old, she is the unconscious oracle through whom prophecy is revealed, the instrument of truth; what she reveals to Seymour is the finality of that unbridgeable gap between human aspiration and human possibility. Seymour's suicide is his summing up.

In part, he would escape the pain that his tattoo, his finite human body, invokes. For this reason Salinger emphasizes it in the final elevator vignette;

the lady with the zinc salve on her nose, like Sybil's and Muriel's mothers and like the daughters themselves, is, however worldly, simple in her failure to suffer. And Seymour, who cannot resent this in a child, is understandably offended when the child-woman rudely reminds him of his pain. But the suicide is also a freeing of the self, for death has its Rilkean, life-extending properties. Seymour's final glance at Muriel—with its echo of a relationship that has failed for him because

> Eines ist, die Geliebte zu singen. Ein anderes, wehe,
> jenen verborgenen schuldigen Fluss-Gott des Bluts.

> One thing to sing the beloved, another, alas!
> that hidden guilty river-god of the blood.[13]

—confirms the hopelessness of his mortal plight; for to love as a man is merely to remind oneself of the limitations of that love. Yet the glance may offer a kind of hope, for perhaps on that shadowy, darker side of life—death—human limitation will give way to infinite possibility. There is little, really, for Seymour to lose. So "he went over and sat down on the unoccupied twin bed, looked at the girl, aimed the pistol, and fired a bullet through his right temple" (p. 26).

Notes

1. Samuel I. Bellman, "New Light on Seymour's Suicide: Salinger's 'Hapworth 16, 1924,'" *Studies in Short Fiction*, 3 (1966), 348.

2. Warren French, *J. D. Salinger* (New York: Twayne, 1963), pp. 82–83.

3. David Galloway, *The Absurd Hero in American Fiction* (Austin, Texas: University of Texas Press, 1970), p. 150.

4. Both Bellman and Galloway, for example, unsatisfied with what "Bananafish" will yield taken alone, look for answers in Salinger's other work. But that work, whatever its merit, cannot explicate a separate story. If "Bananafish" does not provide us sufficient clues to the meaning of its hero's self-destruction, neither *Seymour: An Introduction, Raise High the Roof Beam, Carpenters*, nor "Hapworth 16, 1924" can help it.

5. J. D. Salinger, "A Perfect Day for Bananafish," in *Nine Stories* (Boston: Little, Brown and Co., 1953), p. 7. All further quotations from the story are identified within the text of my essay; all are from this edition.

6. Several critics have suggested Rilke as Seymour's poet, but no one has pursued the implications of that identity. Thus Warren French, for example, in *J. D. Salinger*, p. 80, argues that Rilke's "imagination and sensitivity make it obvious that to Seymour he would be the 'only great poet of the century,'" but French goes no farther than this.

7. Working often from the additional evidence of Salinger's later work, a few critics find Muriel's reading indicative of Seymour's sexual inadequacy. How

difficult it is to make a convincing case for such psychosexual interpretation may be seen in Dallas E. Wiebe, "Salinger's 'A Perfect Day for Bananafish,'" *The Explicator*, 23 (1964), Item 3.

8. Rainer Maria Rilke, *Duino Elegies*, bilingual edition with the translation by J. B. Leishman and Stephen Spender (New York: Norton, 1963), pp. 44–45.

9. The weary eternality of this process is emphasized by the linking of Sybil, Sharon, and "The Waste Land." Eliot's epigraph to the poem and unbearable death-in-life from Petronius, runs thus: "Nam Sibyllam quidem Cumis ego ipse oculis meis vidi in ampulla pendere, et cum illi pueri dicerent: Σίβνλλατί θέλείζ respondebat illa: άγοθαγεϊγ θέλω ["I saw with my own eyes the Cumaen Sybil suspended in a glass bottle, and when the boys would say to her, 'What is the matter, Sybil?' she would answer, 'I long to die.'"] *T. S. Eliot: Collected Poems 1909–1962* (New York: Harcourt Brace, 1963), p. 51.

10. *Duino Elegies*, pp. 22–23.

11. "The Poet," *Emerson: Selected Prose and Poetry*, ed. R. L. Cook (New York: Rinehart, 1965), pp. 327 and 339.

12. "Asides on the Oboe," *The Collected Poems of Wallace Stevens* (New York: Knopf, 1961), pp. 250–251.

13. *Duino Elegies*, pp. 34–35.

.

JAMES LUNDQUIST

A Cloister of Reality: The Glass Family

The important business for the writer of fiction is to place boundaries where, naturally, there are none. A short story or a novel is a limited, formal, artificial representation of the illimitable. The total of consciousness for the writer is like Leibnitz's sea wave whose murmur is made up of all the particular sounds produced by the droplets composing it. As Henry James cautions in the preface to *Roderick Hudson*, "Really, universally, relations stop nowhere, and the exquisite problem of the artist is eternally but *to draw, by a geometry of his own, the circle* within which they shall happily appear to do so."[1] What James means by *circle* is the necessary and arbitrary cutting-out accomplished by the artist in the great fluid mass of experience to create a cloister within which reality can be isolated, contemplated, and represented. For James this comes to be, in a whole series of novels, a matter of establishing a central point of view in the consciousness of a single character and then allowing that point of view to open onto a peripheral world. For Salinger in the work that follows *Nine Stories*, it is a matter of using a family of characters, the Glass family, and multiple—although closely related—points of view in order to delineate the sources of insight and stability that are his way of dealing with and adapting to the chaos of experience.

What seems to happen in Salinger's writing as we read through the later pieces in *Nine Stories*, especially "De Daumier-Smith's Blue Period" and

"Teddy," is that, as much as he is concerned with the exigencies of Zen art, he develops a certain dissatisfaction with the short story form he employs in the earlier parts of the book. He demonstrates considerable impatience with the demands of secondary characterization, dialogues begin turning into monologues, and he violates one rule that Whit Burnett could never have accepted—he does more telling than showing. But this impatience is not with the limitations of the short story so much as it is a symptom of a search for centrality, a search for some means of inventing a universe whose frame will accord with his interpretive fancies in revealing the inner depths of the conscious, illuminated being. This centrality, this universe, finally becomes that of a Jewish-Irish couple and their seven brilliant and generally troubled children, and it is with these characters that Salinger has apparently been chiefly concerned for more than two decades.

In developing the so-called "Glass family saga," Salinger has become more than ever a literary ventriloquist, and he has been soundly (and perhaps deservedly) criticized for this. His tendency even when reproducing a letter written by the sainted Seymour at the age of seven in "Hapworth 16, 1924," is to talk *through* his characters rather than making them seem as if they are speaking *for* themselves. Even so, he does manage to make the members of the Glass family distinct enough so that each of them functions as a means of perceiving things according to the angle of incidence which the separate characters give their creator. At the back of the consciousness of Salinger's Glass family is thus the consciousness of Salinger himself, a little occult at times, and at other times too much in the foreground. To a certain extent, of course, Salinger's writing takes on the qualities of an internal monologue early in his career; but it is only when he centers on the Glass family that the consciousness behind the monologue begins to emerge fully in dialogue with itself, even though many of the themes—the essential obscenity of modern life, the redeeming power of love, the Zen emphasis on transcending the ego—remain the same.

Salinger's interest in the Glass family is not, of course, limited to his last two books and his most recently published story. The most memorable character in *Nine Stories* is the Seymour of "A Perfect Day for Bananafish," his sister, Boo Boo, figures in the much weaker story, "Down at the Dinghy," and Walt Glass's peculiar use of language provides the title for "Uncle Wiggily in Connecticut." In fact, the details about the family are so scattered through Salinger's work that it is necessary for him to outline the family structure by means of a footnote in *Franny and Zooey* (p. 51).[2]

Les Glass and Bessie Gallagher, the parents, were popular Pantages Circuit vaudevillians in the 1920s—a career that has its obvious symbolic implications for the family, because there is a vaudevillian quality to the way Salinger depicts the Glasses. The very way he writes about them, constantly shifting the narrative voice and changing styles, and the way each of the family members is given his or her own genius suggests nothing so much as a stage show consisting of mixed specialty acts, including, songs, dances, comic skits, and even acrobatic performances. By the 1940s, Les (who never figures directly in any of the stories) and Bessie (whose "fat Irish rose" of a personality is very prominent in *Franny and Zooey*) have ended their own performing careers, and Les is working as a talent scout for a motion picture studio in Los Angeles. By the 1950s, when *Franny and Zooey* takes place, they are living in an old but comfortable apartment house in New York (the East Seventies) with their two youngest children.

The oldest, Seymour, has long since committed suicide, but his life does need some recounting. He was born in February 1917, began attending Columbia University when he was fifteen, graduated with a Ph.D. in English, and taught for several years before entering the Army Air Corps. On 4 June 1942, he married a girl named Muriel Fedder, whom he had met while stationed at Fort Monmouth, New Jersey. Possibly because of his reaction to the psychoanalysis he submitted to (under the pressure of Muriel and her mother) after he got out of the Army, he purposely drove the Fedders' car into a tree, and engaged in other bizarre behavior. In the hope that he might recover, he and Muriel took a vacation in Florida, where they had spent their honeymoon. There, as we know from "A Perfect Day for Bananafish," Seymour shot himself on 18 March 1948.

Buddy, the brother with whom Seymour shared a room in his parents' apartment until 1940 (the two brothers then moved into an apartment of their own near 79th and Madison), was born the same year as was Salinger himself (it is significant that Salinger's nickname as a child was "Sonny"), and grew up to be the writer of the family, and Salinger's alter ego, as well. Like Salinger, Buddy never finished college, and he also entered the service when Salinger did, 1942. In 1955 he was a writer in residence teaching in upper New York state at a women's junior college where he lived alone in an unwinterized, unelectrified house.

The first girl born in the family is Boo Boo. As Salinger describes her in "Down at the Dinghy," despite her joke of a name and her lack of prettiness, she is "in terms of permanently memorable, immoderately perceptive, small-area faces—a stunning and final girl" (p. 77). Her adjustment to the world seems remarkable for a Glass child. During the war, when she was a Wave stationed in Brooklyn, she met a steady, businesslike young man named Tannenbaum. By 1955, the Tannenbaums had three children, a summer place somewhere in New England, and a house in Tuckahoe.

The twins, Waker and Walt, were born after Boo Boo, and so far figure less in the family chronicle than even she does. Waker was a conscientious objector during the war, which he spent in a detention camp, and later became a Catholic priest. Walt, as we know from "Uncle Wiggily in Connecticut," spent World War II in the Pacific and was killed in the autumn of 1945 when a Japanese stove he was packing as a souvenir for his commanding officer exploded.

Zachary Martin Glass, known as Zooey, was born in 1929. The handsomest of the Glass children, he became a television actor after he graduated from college, much against the wishes of his mother who wanted him to follow up on his precocious abilities in Mathematics and Greek. Franny, the youngest, born in 1934, is as good-looking as Zooey, and like him is interested in acting, having played summer stock with great success between her junior and senior years in college.

Beginning in 1927 and continuing for seventeen years, at least one and sometimes more of the Glass children was regularly heard on a network radio program, "It's a Wise Child," a children's quiz show. All seven of them, with Seymour, of course, being the most prodigious, astounded their listeners with their ability to answer bookishly cute questions sent in from across the country. As Buddy explains in *Franny and Zooey*, the reaction of the listeners to the performances of the Glass children on the radio show resulted in a division into "two, curiously restive camps: those who held that the Glasses were a bunch of insufferable 'superior' little bastards that should have been drowned or gassed at birth, and those who held that they were bona-fide underage wits and savants, of an uncommon, if unenviable order" (p. 54). This might well be the same division that occurs among Salinger's readers as they get their first extended introduction to the Glass family in *Franny and Zooey*.

The book actually consists of two long stories put together into what almost, but not quite, becomes a novel. An abrupt shift in narrative technique from omniscient point of view in the first story (originally published in *The New Yorker*, 29 January 1955) to having Buddy serve as the narrator in the second (also published in *The New Yorker*, 4 May 1957) gives the book an awkward structure. But despite the narrative shift, the two stories are best considered as one unit, not only because the second story serves to resolve the first, but also because the two of them taken together mark an essential change in Salinger's fiction. Through his use of the Glass family as an organizing concept for his vision, and through his increased reliance on Buddy as the narrator in that portrayal, Salinger attempts to more firmly capture the paradoxical splendor and squalor of life, while concurrently presenting a vision of twentieth-century America that is ultimately positive. The source of that vision is something that comes as a relief after the occasional overemphasis on the efficacy of Oriental thought in *Nine Stories*, and Holden Caulfield's apparent attainment of Buddhahood at the end of *The Catcher in the Rye*.

What we perceive through Salinger's ventriloquial act (his own vaudeville role, so to speak) is a deeper awareness engendered by the paradox itself—that there are no pat answers to the problems of existence—not even Zen—and that the paradox of splendor and squalor, or of the nice and the phony, can be resolved only through character and being. *Franny and Zooey* thus places emphasis on character rather than action, and clearly shows Salinger moving from the well-made structures of his early stories to the discursive narrative insights of Buddy Glass working from his position within the conceptual and focusing frame of the family.[3]

Franny and Zooey opens on the morning of the Yale game at an Ivy League school, with Lane Coutell, a pretentious senior English major of the sort who believes that someday he will own a hotline to *PMLA*, waiting on a railroad platform for Franny, his date for the weekend. Salinger quickly gives us two insights into Lane's character. The first is when one of his classmates in Modern European Literature wants to know what "this bastard Rilke is all about" (p. 6). Lane nonchalantly claims to understand the German-Bohemian poet (1875–1926), but it is soon apparent that someone with Lane's coldness of spirit could never comprehend Rilke's personal soliloquies, the *Duino Elegies*, which celebrate the poet's intense emotional reaction to his existence.[4] The second insight provided by Salinger reinforces the idea of coldness. When Franny's train arrives, Salinger delineates Lane's personality in a sentence that is a reminder of F. Scott Fitzgerald at his best: "Then, like so many people who perhaps ought to be issued only a very probational pass to meet trains, he tried to empty his face of all expressions that might quite simply, perhaps even beautifully, reveal how he felt about the arriving person" (p. 7).

Franny, by contrast, greets Lane warmly, but she immediately feels guilty about expressing affection for him, and Salinger carefully establishes a mood in which both partners sense that everything is unaccountably going wrong with their weekend from the start. They go for lunch to a restaurant called Sickler's, a place where one was careful to order snails, not steak. Lane holds forth pompously, and Franny soon realizes that he epitomizes the self-centered, pseudointellectual qualities that have caused her to become hypersensitive and acutely critical of people like him. "I'm just so sick of pedants and conceited little tearer-downers I could scream," she says (p. 17). They get into an argument over poets and poetry, and in the first of several discussions concerning bad writing versus good writing that is almost a major theme in the last two books, Franny says, "I don't *know* what a real poet is. . . . I know this much, is all. If you're a poet, you do something beautiful. I mean you're supposed to *leave* something beautiful after you get off the page and everything" (p. 19). The poets she knows on the faculty of her college do not do this; they simply leave what she calls "syntax *droppings.*"

This discussion literally makes her sick. She excuses herself from the table and goes to the ladies' room, where she breaks down and cries. She takes a little green book she has been carrying with her out of her purse and presses it to her chest, regaining her composure almost at once. She returns to the table and tries to explain what is bothering her. The main problem is ego and self-centeredness. She tells Lane that she has even dropped out of the play she was in because she could not stand all the ego. "All I know is I'm losing my mind," she tells Lane. "I'm just sick of ego, ego, ego" (p. 29). And then she reluctantly begins to tell him about the little green book, *The Way of a Pilgrim*, written by a Russian peasant in the nineteenth century who wanders across his country until he meets a *starets*, a seer who teaches him a method of praying without ceasing. The method involves repeating the "Jesus Prayer"—"Lord Jesus Christ, have mercy on me"—until the prayer becomes self-active, and *something* happens: "You do it to purify your whole outlook and get an absolutely new conception of what everything's about" (p. 37). The same process is used in Hinduism, Buddhism, and other religions to gain a sense of religious peace and transcend the self, but it means nothing to Lane. As Franny talks about *The Way of a Pilgrim*, he is intent on dissecting the froglegs that are on his plate, and tries to shut her up by asking her if she really believes in that stuff. She replies that it is a way of seeing God: "Something happens in some absolutely nonphysical part of the heart—where the Hindus say that Atman resides, if you ever took any religion—and you see God, that's all" (p. 39). Lane may have taken some religion, but he seems incapable of responding to religious ideas, looks at his watch, and ironically says, "God. We don't have time" (p. 40). He means that they might not be able to get to the game on time, but he also indicates that he has no time for Franny's mysticism concerning apprehending the divine. He tries to tell her that religious experiences of the type she describes all have a simple psychological explanation.

Franny cannot take anymore. She tries to return to the ladies' room but faints before she can get there. She wakes up on a couch in the restaurant manager's office with Lane looking down at her and saying that he is going to take her to the room that he has reserved for her. And then, in his selfishness and blindness (also revealing that they have been lovers), he assures her that he will later try to sneak up the back staircase. He leaves to get a cab, and the first part of the book ends as Franny begins mumbling the Jesus Prayer.

*   *   *

The Way of a Pilgrim and the Jesus Prayer are by no means being put forth as answers to anything by Salinger. Franny has reached the point of a nervous breakdown as Lane leaves her on the couch, and the Jesus Prayer is no solution to her problem. A major idea in Zen (and also in Plato's parable of the cave, and even in Emerson's Perennial Philosophy) is that people who are too critical of others, who are too concerned with the analysis of particulars, fail to reach an understanding of the oneness of all things, and eventually disintegrate themselves.[5] This is what has happened to Franny, and the Jesus Prayer serves only to lead her deeper into her paranoid and hypercritical withdrawal from reality.

The condition Salinger leaves Franny in as she is lying on the couch (a condition that continues on into the second part of the book) indicates that Salinger has become more committed to what might be called the "wait" than to the "quest." Franny is a victim of her fate, not a ruler over it, and her subsequent experience becomes a "downward path to wisdom."[6] From this point on in the story, Salinger pays minimal attention to plot. As in *The Fall* by Camus and *Waiting for Godot* by Beckett, conversation, self-analysis, and the search for meaning within the experience become more important than what happens, and extreme care is exerted to avoid pretending that value exists where it does not.

Franny's search for meaning involves, of course, the dissolution of opposites—good and evil, squalor and splendor, the nice and the phony—that figures so often in Salinger's fiction and is an inevitable result of Salinger's interest in Zen. The Zen neophyte (which so many of his characters, including Franny, resemble) begins by thinking about rational solutions to apparent opposites, including the distinction between self and others, and ultimately reaches an impasse that is created by the struggling ego. When the neophyte "lets go," gives up the struggle, and no longer distinguishes between acting and being acted upon, he is on the way to enlightenment. Once he has reached this state, he is free to be fully acted upon in every action he performs, and this means complete absorption in the process of loss of ego. As we have seen, many of Salinger's stories seem to be structured around producing this experience in some of his characters. Franny is thus a typical Salinger character on the road to enlightenment, wrestling with the problem of burdensome ego, isolated by continual criticism of others and of herself, something that is, in fact, the central dichotomy of the younger Glasses.[7]

But her enlightenment is no simple process and it cannot be seen merely as another dialogue between Zen master and pupil with an easily discernible (if not solvable) *koan* at the center. Nor is it described by means of a tightly structured narrative as her experience in the "Franny" part of the book is. The "Zooey" section is narrated by Buddy, who opens by saying that he is not giving us a short story at all but "a sort of prose home movie" (p. 47), with what plot there is hinging on "mysticism, or religious mystification" (p. 48). The story does have some of the qualities of a home movie because it conveys the impression of an unedited glimpse into the private, and occasionally awkward, moments of life in the Glass household. The idea of the prose home movie is a dangerous metaphor, however, because home movies when viewed at length are finally of interest only to those who see themselves or someone they know intimately on the screen. And the effect often is one of self-indulgence, just the criticism repeatedly directed at Salinger's work from the "Zooey" section on. One does get the feeling in reading the later books that their final charm may be reserved, just as home movies are, for a chosen few or an inner group of initiates. As Buddy says of the leading characters in the story, Franny, Zooey, their mother Bessie, and himself, "We speak a kind of esoteric, family language, a sort of semantic geometry in which the shortest distance between any two points is a fullish circle" (p. 49).

As round-about as the dialogue in the story is, and as esoteric (and precious) as it sometimes seems, it does add up to a ventriloquist's act through which Salinger moves Franny toward a moment of self-transcendence that is as satisfying as anything in his fiction. But the process begins in indirectness and unwinds like an 8 mm film that has been spliced together at the kitchen table. After making his disclaimer at the start, Buddy introduces Zooey, who is reading a four-year-old letter from Buddy, in the bathtub, and Buddy then says that he will refer to himself in the third-person throughout the rest of the story. This does not give us quite the narrative stance that we have in "Franny," however. The presence of Buddy is felt during the rest of the story, and there is a sympathetic, insider's tone that gives the narrative more warmth and authenticity than we find in "Franny."

Buddy reproduces the letter in its entirety, and through it we can see the role he and Seymour played in educating Franny and Zooey—an education Zooey is not altogether satisfied with. After expressing his reservations about Zooey's choice of acting as a career, Buddy tries to explain why he and Seymour took over the instruction of the youngest members of the family so high-handedly. Because of the brilliance of Franny and Zooey on the quiz show, both Seymour and Buddy began to worry that the two child prodigies would turn into "academic weisenheimers." Seymour had become convinced, through his reading in Zen, that education should not begin with a quest for knowledge but with a quest for "no-knowledge," the realization that the state of pure consciousness known as *satori* involves being with God before he said, "Let there be light." So the prescribed reading included Max Mueller's *Sacred Books of the East*, and Franny and Zooey grew up knowing more about Jesus and Gautama and Lao-tse and Shankaracharya and Huineng and Sri Ramakrishna than they did about Homer or Shakespeare or George Washington. All of this had so much impact on Zooey at one time that he tried to get over an unhappy love affair by translating the Mundaka Upanishad into classical Greek.

Buddy apologizes for not following up on this early instruction after the death of Seymour, and explains that what prompted the letter was hearing a little girl in a supermarket say she has two boyfriends, "Bobby and Dorothy." This reminded him of Seymour's observation that all legitimate religious study leads to unlearning the illusory differences between boys and girls, day and night, and heat and cold. But this is not easy to unlearn, and the instruction has hardly been beneficial to Franny and Zooey—Franny has suffered an incipient nervous breakdown and Zooey has an ulcer.

Zooey puts the letter away and picks up a script for a television play he has been reading, when Bessie, dressed in a kimono and a hairnet, comes into the bathroom and opens the medicine cabinet. Here we are given a long list of what is in the cabinet—from Ex-Lax to three tickets to a 1946 musical comedy, "Call Me Mister." The list is distracting and does not seem necessary, but it functions (as do the later catalogs of the contents of the Glass family living room and the bulletin-board collection of famous quotations in Seymour and Buddy's room) not only to continue the prose home movie idea, but also to emphasize that there are objects, furnishings, and ideas that have an existence—are *there*—independent of the internalized concerns of the ego. This cataloging tendency continues through the next book and emphasizes the point that while it is necessary to see through external reality, it is still there, still real, and must be dealt with before any transcendence can take place.

Zooey carries on a long and irritable conversation with his mother from behind the bath curtain (another example of Salinger characters not addressing each other directly—it is as if there is a bath curtain separating all of them). Bessie is a great worrier, but her worry at the moment concerns Franny. Bessie wants Zooey to find out what is bothering his sister. Since she got home on Saturday night (it is now Monday morning), she has kept to the couch, has been unable to eat, and remains silent and withdrawn. Bessie does suspect, however, that the little green book might have something to do with Franny's condition, and Zooey indicates that she could not have made a better guess. He tells her that the book and a sequel to it, "The Pilgrim Continues His Way," came out of Seymour and Buddy's bedroom, and it is because of Seymour and Buddy's educational system that both he and Franny are especially susceptible to such ideas. "We're *freaks*, the two of us, Franny and I," he announces. "I'm a twenty-five-year-old freak and she's a twenty-year-old freak, and both those bastards are responsible. . . . The symptoms are a little more delayed in Franny's case than mine, but she's a freak, too, and don't you forget it. I swear to you, I could murder them both without even batting an eyelash. The great teachers. The great emancipators. My God. I can't even sit down to lunch with a man any more and hold up my end of a decent conversation" (pp. 103–104). And he adds that he cannot even sit down to a meal without first saying "The Four Great Vows" of Buddhism under his breath: "However innumerable beings are, I vow to save them; however inexhaustible the passions are, I vow to extinguish them; however immeasurable the Dharmas are, I vow to master them; however incomparable the Buddha-truth is, I vow to attain it" (pp. 104–105). Instead of being enlightening, the four vows have become obsessive.

With this attitude, Zooey ends his talk with Bessie, gets dressed, and goes into the living room to wake Franny up. Near the start of the dialogue, Zooey notices some sheet music on a stand. A sepia reproduction of Mr. and Mrs. Glass in top hat and tails is featured on the cover, and the title, "You Needn't Be So Mean, Baby," functions for Zooey as a beatific signal. He tells Franny that one problem with both of them is that they have "Wise Child" complexes, that they both cannot stop picking at others because of their own sense of superiority. He accuses her of using the Jesus Prayer for egotistical purposes, for laying up spiritual treasures for herself, without even praying to the "real" Jesus. He reminds her of the time when she was ten and came rushing into his room with a Bible in her hand saying she could no longer believe in Jesus because of the way he threw the tables around in the synagogue and because he said that human beings are more valuable to God than the fowls of the air. At that point, Zooey says, she quit the Bible and went straight to Buddha because of her inability to understand any son of God who might actually have said and done the things attributed to him. And now in using the name Jesus as a *mantra* in the Jesus Prayer with the idea, recognized in most meditative religions, that repetition of a word or phrase until it is automatic will lead to escape from external reality, she is continuing that tendency. But the Jesus Prayer that Jesus himself might have advocated would have a different aim—"To endow the person who says it with Christ-Consciousness. *Not* to set up some little cozy, holier-than-thou trysting place with some sticky, adorable divine *pers*onage who'll take you in his arms and relieve you of all your duties and make all your nasty *Weltschmerzen* ... go away and never come back" (p. 172). Wholesale adoption of the Jesus Prayer as a mantra is dangerous, Zooey explains, because it is entirely possible for someone to be blissfully reciting it while robbing the poorbox. Real Christ-Consciousness involves the realization that "You Needn't Be So Mean, Baby."

What Zooey is getting at here is the old problem of dichotomies in Salinger's thought. Religious mysticism can be nice, but it can also be phony. At the time the stories were written, Zen had become not only fashionable but downright faddish as had other mystical ways of seeking transcendence, and the dialogue between Franny and Zooey seems clearly to be a reaction to this phenomenon. Seymour may have reached the state of enlightenment through his studies in Oriental wisdom, and Buddy may nearly have gotten there, but for Franny it has led to a breakdown and for Zooey an anxiety-caused illness. What Salinger is doing is something that seems inevitable in American thought. He is cautioning that we must take pragmatism into account in judging any religious approach or philosophical notion. We should ask the question, does it work? Simple mysticism simply accepted does not. Nor does an educational approach that *forces* the learning of the East on unsuspecting subjects as the young Franny and Zooey were.

Retreat from external reality, whether it be undertaken simple-mindedly through the Jesus Prayer or the necessity of it forced upon us by would-be gurus, can be just as phony as blindly pursuing material wealth and pleasure. And besides, Zooey realizes that external reality is not always so bad, and it is a mistake to lose touch with it. In the midst of his discussion with Franny, Zooey looks out the window and sees a little girl playing a trick on her dachshund. She is hiding behind a tree waiting for the dog to pick up her scent and find her. When the dog does, the two experience an immense and playful reunion. Zooey cannot help saying, "God damn it, there are nice things in the world—and I mean *nice* things. We're all such morons to get so sidetracked. Always, always, always referring every goddam thing that happens right back to our lousy little egos" (p. 152).

Franny starts to cry, and Zooey realizes he is not getting anywhere with her, perhaps because he is being too critical. He goes into Seymour and Buddy's room, where Seymour's separate-listing telephone has been kept all these years. He sits in front of the telephone with a white handkerchief on his head and thinks for awhile. Then he picks up the phone, dials the apartment telephone, disguises his voice as Buddy's, and asks to speak to Franny. He makes use of his acting ability not to draw attention to himself, nor to flatter his own ego as most actors do, but instead he acts out of kindness, out of concern for Franny. He thinks it will help her if she can hear Buddy's voice, but he makes a slip and she recognizes him. He tells her that she can go on with the Jesus Prayer, that he has no right to criticize her, but that she should realize that the only thing that counts in religious life of any sort is *detachment* and selflessness. But she should realize that "desirelessness" is not the same thing and is not necessarily good. It is her desiring to be an actress that has made her a good one. "You're stuck with it now," he reminds her. "You can't just *walk out* on the results of your own hankerings. Cause and effect, buddy, cause and effect" (p. 198). So what can she do? For her, he says, the only religious thing she can do is to *act*: "Act for God, if you want to—be God's actress, if you want to" (p. 198). But what she cannot do is act for herself, for her own ego, or even rave about the stupidity of the audiences. She has to act selflessly in the theatre, the world, as it is. This is part of Christ-Consciousness, something the Jesus Prayer can never give her.

He tries to explain to her what this means in another way by telling her how he resisted shining his shoes before one performance of "It's a Wise Child" because he thought the studio audience, the announcer, and the sponsors were all morons. Not only that, his shoes could not even be seen by the audience from where he sat. Seymour heard all this and told him to shine them anyway, to shine them for the "Fat Lady." Seymour did not tell him who she was, and Zooey had a picture in his mind of a cancerous woman sitting on her porch all day swatting flies and listening to the radio, but it somehow all made sense to him, and he shined his shoes. Franny confesses that Seymour had said the same thing to her. Zooey says to her that he is going to tell her a terrible secret. "*There isn't anyone out there who isn't Seymour's Fat Lady*," he says. "That includes your Professor Tupper, buddy. And all his goddam cousins by the dozens. There isn't anyone *any*where that isn't Seymour's Fat Lady. Don't you know that? Don't you know that goddam secret yet? And don't you know—*listen* to me, now—*don't you know who that Fat Lady really is?* . . . Ah, buddy. Ah, buddy. It's Christ Himself. Christ Himself, buddy" (pp. 201–202).

This emphasis on the need to give love to others, on the need to practice a selfless and lonely benevolence, gives Franny a sudden moment of joy, a *satori* based not on retreat from external reality but of acceptance of her place within it. Like the Sergeant at the end of "For Esmé—with Love and Squalor," she falls into a deep dreamless sleep, the squalor in her life resolved through love.

*   *   *

But we must be careful in reading this story not to assume that Salinger is naively advocating the acceptance of Christianity through Zooey's long discussion of the nature of Christ and the incarnation of Jesus in the Fat Lady. If we look at the story this way, as an argument for Christianity, the resolution of Franny's breakdown at the end appears to be too sudden and without clear explanation. It is difficult to see how Zooey's theological and ethical arguments, taken simply by themselves, could bring about a conversion in anyone as intelligent as Franny is. We must remember, however, that despite his attack on the Jesus Prayer, Salinger is still writing with the Zen ideas found in *Nine Stories* in mind, although considerably more cautiously expressed, in *Franny and Zooey*. What happens at the end of the book is quite in keeping with Zen teachings. Zen enlightenment is often the result of a ridiculous gesture of the master or an absurd answer to a serious question. So one way of understanding the ending is to realize that Franny gets over her break-down by the very absurdity of Zooey's equation of Christ and the Fat Lady.[8] Salinger thus does not prescribe an all-encompassing love for the predicament of modern man, but suggests that the solution lies in the Christ-Consciousness that is the result of enlightenment through absurdity.

This positive view of the possibilities for enlightenment amid the splendor and squalor of modern life does not depend, however, on an acceptance of either the ideas of Zen or the beliefs of Christianity. It is a statement in favor of seeking the ultimate solution through character. *Franny and Zooey* lacks overt rendering of action. In fact, the single most dramatic action is Franny's falling asleep at the end. But through dialogue, Salinger has Buddy show us how Franny moves away from the pat answer of the Jesus Prayer to the moment of release when she overcomes the problem of ego. Her enlightenment represents a growth in character that is permitted and encouraged by the family circle within which it takes place and which affords a range of possibilities. "Everybody in this family gets his goddam religion in a different package," Zooey says (p. 154). But the problem for all of them is to deal with hyper-criticism, with the ego. And this is the message they all apparently sooner or later discover out of the legacy of Seymour's wisdom and the fact of his suicide.

* * *

The message does not arrive very speedily or with much economy of statement. And the same commentary might be made on the entire "Zooey" part of the book that is made about the letter from Buddy that is read in the bathtub: "virtually endless in length, overwritten, teaching, repetitious, opinionated, remonstrative, condescending, embarrassing—and filled to a surfeit with affection" (p. 56). It is difficult to defend the book structurally other than to use Buddy's metaphor of the prose home movie (a metaphor that implies a lack of structure), and the book did come as something of an embarrassment to readers who had defended and admired the earlier books. But *Franny and Zooey* has an unusual quality in contemporary fiction—it deals with characters the author actually *likes*. At times there may indeed be a surfeit of affection, but the affection nonetheless is transferable to the reader. Earnestness is, of course, no justification for a lack of style and structure, but the narrative warmth that comes through this book justifies Salinger's use of the Glass family as a means of delineating the sources and range of his insight and stability.

Salinger's love for the Glasses left some reviewers uneasy, however. John Updike, for instance, writing in the *New York Times Book Review*, objected to the uncomplementary jangle of the book's two parts, and then complained that "Salinger loves the Glasses ... too exclusively. ... He loves them to the detriment of artistic moderation."[9] And in stronger language, Alfred Kazin went at much the same thing in the *Atlantic*. The Glass children are not only "cute," he wrote, but they "do not trust anything or anyone but themselves and their great idea. And what troubles me about this is not what it reflects of their theology but what it does to Salinger's art."[10]

But just as many, if not more, critics were taken by the book's warmth, although the seeming lack of control remained disturbing. *Time* responded to Kazin's charge by stating, "Critics . . . have suggested that the Glass children are too cute and too possessed by self-love. The charge is unjust. They are too clearly shadowed by death, even in their wooliest, most kittenish moments, to be cute, and they are too seriously worried about the very danger of self-love to be true egotists."[11] The very tenderness of the book appealed to the reviewer in *The Christian Century*: "The cumulative effect is bright and tender rather than powerful, and poignant rather than deep: these are the strengths and limitations of Salinger as a writer. These granted, he has an almost Pauline understanding of the necessity, nature, and redemptive quality of love. In Salinger, probably more than in any other serious contemporary writer of fiction, the modern college generation seems to find a mirror of its problems."[12] It was the treatment of love that also impressed A. E. Mayhew in *Commonweal*: "These two stories are about love. . . . For all their faults, they have a pleasing toughness and positiveness in their intent, something more than the verbal sleight-of-hand for which Salinger is justly famous."[13] Granville Hicks, in *The Saturday Review*, replied to the many attacks on the book by writing that "Some critics have charged him with priggishness, and have said that he always has to put his heroes and heroines in the right. This is manifestly untrue. He dares to create characters who have virtue as their goal, but both Franny and Zooey are agonizingly conscious of their shortcomings, and both have a horror of self-righteousness. . . . In *Franny and Zooey* he is at the top of his form."[14]

*   *   *

Hicks was one of the few critics who could come out so glowingly for *Franny and Zooey*. The hesitations over Salinger's sudden prolixity were behind most of the reactions to the book, and many commentators flatly did not like what they sensed to be a shift in Salinger's narrative technique. Most of these hesitations were validated, so it seemed, when *Raise High the Roof Beam, Carpenters; and Seymour: An Introduction* was published in 1963. This is partly because the book is somewhat similar in structure to *Franny and Zooey*. The first section consists of a story (originally published in *The New Yorker*, 19 November 1955) complete with plot and even something of a resolution, and the second section (*The New Yorker*, 6 June 1959) is a dialogue of sorts between Buddy and Seymour (or rather, Seymour's ghost) that serves peripherally as a commentary on the first story, provides us, as the title indicates, with more information on Seymour, and finally comes down to a discussion of the nature of art, the crucial differences between poetry and prose, and the predicament of the artist. But even though both sections are this time narrated by Buddy, the two parts of the book do not fit together tightly, and "Seymour: An Introduction" comes about as close to being an essay as a piece of fiction can. However, the overall effect is one of intended delight. As in *Franny and Zooey*, Salinger is clearly writing about characters for whom he feels great affection because of the way they provide him with a means of centralizing his vision. And the antiform style that emerges in "Zooey" and to a much greater extent in "Seymour" need not be seen as a negative development or as "the self-indulgence of a writer flirting with depths of wisdom."[15] Ihab Hassan suggests a useful approach in pointing out that Salinger's later style may be understood as a metaphor of his sacramental and celebrational view of life: a work of art is an act of faith, and the act itself is a celebration."[16]

Indeed, "Raise High the Roof Beam, Carpenters" centers on sacrament and celebration, although ironically at first. It deals with Seymour's wedding to Muriel, but Seymour does not appear, and Buddy, the only member of the Glass family who is able to be present for the ceremony, is forced into a car with four other wedding guests to be driven to the apartment of the bride's parents for what has turned out to be a non-wedding reception." The situation Salinger utilizes to build his story around is a classic one in vaudeville and burlesque humor (First woman: "I heard you had a lovely wedding." Second woman: "Yes, it was wonderful. I was so happy. But it would have been even lovelier had my husband showed up"). Salinger makes the most of the humorous possibilities in Buddy's predicament with the other guests, one of whom is the Matron of Honor, not knowing at first who he is. The Matron of Honor is, of course, incensed at Seymour and talks on and on about how Muriel's mother ought now to be more than ever convinced that Seymour is a latent homosexual and a schizoid personality. What kind of a man, she asks, would keep his bride up until five in the morning the day of the wedding, as Seymour reportedly did, to tell her he is too *happy* to get married? Buddy's uncomfortable response to this line of conversation makes the Matron of Honor suspicious, and she guesses that he is Seymour's brother.

The car is stopped by a policeman to let a detail of Sea Scouts march by, and as the delay continues and the heat inside the car becomes unbearable, the passengers decide to walk to a nearby Schrafft's for a soda. Buddy learns that one of the other guests, a little old man who sits staring straight ahead with an unlit cigar in his mouth and a top hat on his head, is a deaf mute. They have to write him a note to ask if he wants to go along. He answers with one word: "Delighted." The Schrafft's is closed for alterations, so Buddy invites the others to his air-conditioned apartment, just a few blocks away, to escape the heat. When they get there, Buddy can stand the Matron of Honor's criticisms no longer, and he tells her that no one has seen Seymour for what he is—a poet. The Matron of Honor's only response is to ask if she can use the telephone so she can call the Fedders and explain the delay. In showing her into the bedroom where the telephone is, Buddy sees Seymour's diary and picks it up. He goes into the bathroom with it and there sees wedding congratulations written by Boo Boo (she had been staying in the apartment while Buddy and Seymour, both in the service, were at their army posts) in soap on the mirror. The message, which gives the story its title, is a verse from Sappho: "Raise high the roof beams, carpenters. Like Ares comes the bridegroom, taller far than a tall man" (p. 76). What follows next is a reproduction of parts of the diary, which was written when Seymour was stationed at Fort Monmouth in late 1941 and early 1942. Buddy is somewhat dismayed to learn that Seymour loves Muriel for her "undiscriminating heart." It is her lack of ego, her willingness to be uncritical that Seymour likes about her—a lesson that Buddy as narrator had not yet learned. Seymour writes about the growing suspicion Mrs. Fedder has that he is a schizoid personality. She is particularly disturbed over his reply to her question about what he intended to do when the war was over. His answer: He would like to be a dead cat. Mrs. Fedder thought he was making some kind of sophisticated joke, and her laughter distracted Seymour so much that he forgot to explain what he meant. He later told Muriel the point of the remark was that, as a Zen master once said, a dead cat is the most valuable thing in the world because no one could put a price on it.

Mrs. Fedder's suspicions continue to grow despite Muriel's explanation to her of what Seymour had actually meant by the dead-cat business, and she arranges to have her analyst present for dinner one night when Seymour is there. The analyst grills Seymour, coming down finally to a question about why Seymour was forced off "It's a Wise Child." The analyst had the impression that Seymour had said over the air that the Gettysburg Address was harmful to children. What he had said is that it is a bad speech for children to have to memorize because there had been 51,112 casualties at Gettysburg, and that if someone had to speak, the only appropriate response would have been to shake his fist at the audience and walk off the platform. Out of love for Muriel and to set Mrs. Fedder at ease, Seymour does agree to submit to psychoanalysis, but he has already diagnosed his condition: "Oh, God, if I'm anything by a clinical name, I'm a kind of paranoiac in reverse. I suspect people of plotting to make me happy" (p. 88).

Buddy slams the diary shut at the word *happy*. He feels betrayed, and there is more than a hint of jealousy in his reaction to the news that Seymour actually loves Muriel, and that he looks upon his marriage as almost a rebirth through the assumption of responsibility. Boo Boo in her wedding note intuitively indicates that she recognizes Seymour's motive as a desire to share the life of common mortals—but she also indicates something more ominous, that ordinary life and institutions will have to be generously expanded (the roofbeams raised) to accommodate the heroic proportions of Seymour. But Buddy as a writer of fiction instinctively reacts against this idea because he cannot believe in a happy ending so easily achieved.

When we first encounter Seymour in "A Perfect Day for Bananafish," we wonder how he could ever have married Muriel. In "Raise High the Roof Beam, Carpenters," we can understand how it happened, but we are also led to think of a few literary parallels involving the love-matches of genius-heroes—King Arthur and Guinevere, Dante and Beatrice, Faust and Gretchen, and, probably the most direct parallel, Gatsby and Daisy. In all of these examples, the hero is attracted to a woman who represents innocence and purity that is perceived by the lover, at any rate, as a lack of ego and a willingness to love him wholly and freely despite the burden of genius. And in every case, the consequences are disastrous. Mundane life is mundane life and cannot be expanded to accommodate the hero. External reality, as Zooey tells Franny, is inescapably *there*, and the tragedy of genius is to assume that it can be altered.

Many readers of Salinger have assumed that Seymour is to be understood as an unquestioned saint within the Glass family, a seer whose wisdom is final. To be certain, his personality, his diaries, his poems, his sayings, are with every member of the Glass family all the time, but not always as a positive force. Zooey and Buddy are in the process of rebelling *against* Seymour. In one sense, Seymour's suicide is justifiable. It is entirely acceptable within the Zen context *Nine Stories* provides. But outside of that context and from the point-of-view of Zooey, an actor, and Buddy, a writer, it becomes tragic. Seymour makes the same mistake Gatsby does—he idealizes a woman and isolates her conceptually from the reality that surrounds her. Gatsby overlooks the fact of Daisy's marriage and wants to ignore the existence of her daughter. Seymour discounts the presence of Muriel's family, especially her mother, and fails to see what they will do to him—they will not raise the roof beam; they intend to lower it.

The whole concept of Seymour as a Gatsby-figure is reinforced by the atmosphere of the gathering in Buddy's apartment. It is similar to the scene in *The Great Gatsby* where Gatsby, Daisy, Tom, Jordon, and Nick motor in from Long Island on a hot summer day and spend the afternoon drinking in the parlor of a suite in the Plaza Hotel room. The discussion revolves around the idea of happiness, and Gatsby's unwillingness to face reality is contrasted by Tom's matter-of-fact attitude that what is, is, and we can no more will to be happy than we can bring the past back.

Buddy emerges from the bathroom, serves his guests some Tom Collinses, and belts down several shots of whiskey. The Matron of Honor returns from the telephone and says all is well, Seymour and Muriel have eloped. All of the guests leave except the little old man who raises his glass to Buddy in salute. He suddenly becomes a symbol of death, reminiscent of the old man at the crossroads in Chaucer's "The Pardoner's Tale," grinning indifferently as Buddy tries to explain and justify Seymour's peculiar behavior. Buddy passes out, a premonition of Seymour's tragedy hanging over him. When he awakens, the old man is gone, the only trace of his presence an empty glass and a cigar end in a pewter ashtray. "I still think his cigar end should have been forwarded on to Seymour, the usual run of wedding gifts being what it is," Buddy concludes. "Just the cigar, in a small, nice box. Possibly with a blank sheet of paper enclosed, by way of explanation" (p. 107).

The empty glass and the cigar end function the same way as do the beatific signs in the earlier stories, but here the import is more subtle. Buddy achieves understanding at the end of "Raise High the Roof Beam, Carpenters," but it is not the kind that allows him to drift off into a dreamless and restorative sleep as do Sergeant X and Franny. The word *glass* is a crucial one for Buddy to use at the end, because he is not seeing through the glass the way Daumier-Smith looks through the window in a blaze of illumination. Buddy is seeing through the glass darkly as he realizes the difficulties in understanding the meaning of Seymour's presence in his own life and in that of his brothers and sisters. But as the glass darkens, the pattern of Salinger's saga of the Glass family becomes more clear. Seymour is a catalyst who changes others but does not himself undergo change. He teaches Buddy, Zooey, and Franny to be realists, naturalists, and humanists, even though he is a Zen-master, mystic, seer, and Christ-figure himself, with standards so high, so out-of-this-world that he cannot survive.[17] He is also a fool, a Gatsby-type who, through his fatal example, teaches the other characters that they must move toward compromise if they are to have a philosophy they can live by.

* * *

It is the idea of compromise that Buddy is mulling over at the age of forty when "Seymour: An Introduction" begins. He is speculating about his own career as a writer, a career that at first does seem like a considerable compromise when contrasted to that of Seymour. Buddy is a writer of fiction who must worry about communicating with the "general reader." Seymour, on the other hand, was a poet, a *mukta*, an enlightened man, a "true artist-seer, the heavenly fool who can and does produce beauty, [and] is mainly dazzled to death by his own scruples" (p. 123). What Buddy does in the long, rambling monologue that follows is to define his and Seymour's contrasting temperaments, and also to attempt the resolution of the contradictory impulses that beset the artist. Because of his very genius, his talent and sensitivity, the artist stands apart from the common lot of men. This is certainly Seymour's case, and he made no attempt to publish his poetry (Buddy has one of Seymour's notebooks with 184 poems in it—all the poems greatly influenced by Chinese and Japanese tradition, of course). But if the artist submits his work to the public, it is another matter. And this is Buddy's case. Once he publishes and performs before his audience, he involves himself in their lives and is forced to acknowledge a responsibility to others.

Buddy's agonizing over problems in communication, his relationship to his reader, and the writer's inherent moral dilemma also is Salinger's. This is underscored by the two quotations that precede the story, one by Kafka, one by Kierkegaard. The quotation from Kafka is:

> The actors by their presence always convince me, to my horror, that most of what I've written about them until now is false. It is false because I write about them with steadfast love (even now, while I write it down, this, too, becomes false) but varying ability, and this varying ability does not hit off the real actors loudly and correctly but loses itself dully in this love that never will be satisfied with the ability and therefore thinks it is protecting this ability from exercising itself. (p. 111)

This is Kafka at his paradoxical and contradictory best (or worst), but what he is saying is something that comes out more and more as Salinger writes about the Glass family. That is, the characters of a writer, once created, take on a reality of their own that the writer must respect even to the point of protecting it from his own craft, which through its very artifice can falsify. Salinger's love for his characters overwhelms his simple storytelling techniques and encourages the personae of the Glass family to emerge all the more convincingly. The writer's craft is, as it were, broken by his own creation; but when this happens, his vision takes on new largeness and strangeness. It is not easy to predict what "Seymour: An Introduction" is to lead toward, but Helen Weinberg comments, "The story is governed by a sense of breakthrough and experiment."[18]

The quotation from Kierkegaard further enunciates the nature of Salinger's breakthrough:

> It is (to describe it figuratively) as if an author were to make a slip
> of the pen, and as if this clerical error became conscious of being
> such. Perhaps this was no error, but in a far higher sense was an
> essential part of the whole exposition. It is, then, as if this clerical
> error were to revolt against the author, out of hatred for him, were
> to forbid him to correct it, and were to say, "No, I will not be erased,
> I will not be erased, I will stand as a witness against thee, that thou
> art a very poor writer. (p. 149)

The "slip" apparently is Seymour, whose creation in "A Perfect Day for Bananafish" and his subsequent suicide may well have been an "accident" (the suddenness of the ending and its inexplicable quality the first time one reads the story is some hint that Salinger may have hit on it by "error" or chance). But accident or not, a presence was created who cannot be dispelled. And the ghost of Seymour does haunt Salinger's writing as much as it does the minds of the Glass family survivors. Salinger indicates as much by making details of Buddy's life correspond to his own, thus stressing the complicated relationship between character and author.

Something that should also be kept in mind here is that the idea of the "controlled accident" is important in Zen art. A work of art is regarded as not only representing nature but as being itself a work of nature. Zen paintings, for example, are supposed to be formed as naturally as the hills and trees they depict. This does not mean that art should be left to mere chance and that the artist so forget about control that his work becomes chaos. "The point," stresses Watts, "is rather that for Zen there is no duality, no conflict between the natural element of chance and the human element of control. The constructive powers of the human mind are no more artificial than the formative actions of plants or bees, so that from the standpoint of Zen it is no contradiction to say that artistic technique is discipline in spontaneity and spontaneity in discipline."[19] The whole question thus becomes one for Salinger of whether or not such a concept of Zen art can work as fictional technique.

The quotations from Kafka and Kierkegaard along with the corresponding implications of Zen art do suggest one thing—that the entire story is a fictional treatise on the artistic process. Instead of being concerned with the story itself as a final product, Salinger focuses on the process and the *consequences* of the process of creation. He is writing the story of Buddy as a writer while simultaneously writing his own story as a writer, and the key to both becomes a matter of process, change, and eventual illumination, the *satori* being the artist's own sudden understanding of what his art is, what it can do, and what his relationship to it is. This is what Seymour means when he tells Buddy that writing cannot be a profession; it must be a religion.

But Buddy must struggle with the differences between himself and Seymour, the differences between poetry and fiction. Buddy's writing differs from Seymour's, and his religion must differ also. In speaking through Buddy, Salinger allows a distinction between poetry and fiction much like Edgar Allan Poe's discrimination—the poet is a higher order of moral being. Buddy cities a Zen story about how a seer is able to choose a horse by seeing through its external qualities to its ideal nature; and this is just what Seymour could do. He could perceive the essential, inward qualities of the spiritual mechanism. But as a fiction writer, Buddy seems incapable of the selflessness necessary to achieve Seymour's vision. The fiction writer must create characters that come out of himself, out of his ego. How, therefore, can he lose his ego without destroying his art? The more he gets involved in his characters, the more he gets involved in himself, and he cannot hope to experience the illumination of the poet who loses himself in the poetic current that runs through things. All Buddy can learn from Seymour, finally, is that the secret or art is to become fully yourself by putting your whole heart into a work. This is not the way of a saint, but it is what the artist can learn from the saint.

*   *   *

Critical reaction to *Raise High the Roof Beam, Carpenters; and Seymour: An Introduction* was, understandably, mixed. Many critics were simply not willing to accept the form or the language of the book. "Hopelessly prolix," Irving Howe objected in the *New York Times Book Review*. "With their cozy parentheses and clumsy footnotes, their careening mixture of Jewish vaudeville humor and Buddhist prescription, they betray a loss of creative discipline, a surrender to cherished mannerisms. And as the world of Salinger comes more fully into view, it seems increasingly open to critical attack. It is hard to believe in Seymour's saintliness, hard even to credit him as a fictional character, for we are barely able to see him at all behind the palpitations of Buddy's memory."[20] John Wain, writing in the *New Republic*, found Salinger's use of Buddy as narrator impossible: "Buddy is a bore. He is prolix, obsessed with his subject, given to rambling confidences, and altogether the last person to be at the helm in an enterprise like this."[21] And in an article in *Twentieth Century Literature*, Paul Levine voiced a widely held objection to Salinger's techniques in his later work: "they blur the distance between the author and his subject matter. This lack of aesthetic distance creates a personal interplay between author and character rather than between character and character. The stories hold the reader's attention not through the revelation of character but through the revelation of author, reducing Salinger's audience to his aficionados and troubled adolescents in general."[22]

But some reviewers were able to assess Salinger's experimentation more appreciatively, and more correctly, although not without some reservations. "The reader should appreciate the artistry in Salinger's deftness of diction, sureness of touch, clearness of tone," J. J. Quinn wrote in *Best Sellers*. "This is particularly important for the latter piece, 'the long, agonizing prose poem,' sounding observations on Life, Character, and the Vocation of the literary artist. The style may get in the way of a reader who mistakes an essay for a short story. The tone may puzzle many. . . . [but] Mature readers will marvel at the brilliant performance that marks the unmistakable Salinger style in presenting his remarkable Glass family."[23] As wild as Buddy's words run, Salinger does show him realizing his atonement at last, even though form must be shattered to do so in making garrulousness a virtue, a necessity, rather than a defect. "My opinion is that Salinger, in clownish guise, has sought to inhibit the profane impulse of language by indulging language prodigally," Ihab Hassan wrote in one of his unusually insightful observations. "The comic battle Salinger wages against language is also the tragic battle man fights with eternity. No one in recent fiction has accepted more difficult terms for that battle than Salinger. It is to our honor that he persists in it with love and grace."[24]

*   *   *

Salinger's battle extends to at least one more story, "Hapworth 16, 1924," which appeared in *The New Yorker*, 19 June 1965, and which shows Salinger still struggling with Seymour's haunting presence. Buddy, now at age forty-six, tries to trace the origins of his older brother's saintliness in a letter Seymour wrote home from Camp Simon Hapworth in Maine when he was seven. In giving us the exact copy of the letter, Buddy provides us with the fullest example we yet have of things as seen from Seymour's point-of-view, and we are thoroughly introduced to the sensitivity and psychic powers that foreshadow his spirituality. We are also exposed to an incredibly precocious mind that soon becomes revolting. Incredibly advanced for his age (or for any age), Seymour writes about how the other boys at camp, and their counselors as well, are slated to go through life with "picayune, stunted attitudes toward everything in the universe and beyond."[25] He mentions that he has developed a "sensual attraction" (at the age of seven, yet) to a Mrs. Happy (it is, as we have seen, his desire for happiness that may be his tragic flaw), the pregnant wife of the camp manager. He tells how Buddy, also at the camp, managed to obtain the use of the mess hall for reading and studying by betting the man in charge, Mr. Nelson, that he can memorize, within a half-hour, a book Mr. Nelson has been reading, *Hardwoods of North America* (Buddy does it). He reflects on the nature of pain: "Half the pain around, unfortunately, quite belongs to somebody else who either shirked it or did not know how to grasp it firmly by the handle."[26] And he asks his parents to send him some books by Tolstoy, Vivekananda of India, Dickens, George Eliot, Thackeray, Austen, Bunyan, and Porter Smith (*Chinese Materia Medica*), among others.

In this story, Salinger attempts to portray Seymour in the process of deepening his awareness. Seymour's special powers and his special weaknesses apparently must be thought of as emanating from some central force underlying all changing manifestations of reality. But the character that emerges is monstrous, fully as hideous in some ways, as the devil-children in such recent movies as *The Omen*. What the story does is to emphasize how oppressive as well as potentially enlightening Seymour's influence on his brothers and sisters must be. He is a grotesque, but then so are the lives of most saints.

"Hapworth," along with Salinger's last two books, marked a long pause that some readers believe may indicate a dead-end for Salinger. Stanley Edgar Hyman's reaction to *Raise High the Roof Beam, Carpenters; and Seymour: An Introduction* is that Salinger has gotten himself into a cul-de-sac: "His highway has turned into a dirt road, then into wagon ruts, finally into a squirrel track and climbed a tree."[27] But Salinger's final phase, to date, certainly indicates more than that. Not only does his treatment of the Glass family and the problem of Seymour as a character give us clues to the imaginative impulse Salinger has struggled with; it may also serve as a dramatization of the creative process itself. Salinger has invented for himself a cloister within which his own consciousness can be isolated, contemplated, and represented, but he has done something else as well: He has created a set of characters who comprise a real family full of love and concern for one another, a family whose story may not be complete (and may never be completed), and a family that presents the same demands on the reader that Faulkner's McCaslin family does—that is, the reader must reconstruct much of the genealogy and family history from scattered allusions. But it is a family whose fictional presence enlarges itself like a spot of oil in the consciousness of the reader as through it we darkly apprehend those sources of insight and substantiality that may enable us to do what Buddy would have us do—come to terms with ourselves and the only world we have.

NOTES

1. Henry James, "Preface," *Roderick Hudson*, New York Edition of the Novels and Tales of Henry James, I (New York: Scribner's, 24 vols., 1907–17), viii.

2. J. D. Salinger, *Franny and Zooey* (New York: Bantam, 1964). All subsequent page references are to this edition.

3. For a further discussion of this change in Salinger, see Sam S. Baskett, "The Splendid/Squalid World of J. D. Salinger," *Wisconsin Studies in Contemporary Literature*, Winter 1963, pp. 48–61.

4. Salinger mentions Rilke several times in his fiction, and there are more than a few parallels between the lives of the two writers—both had apparently unhappy experiences in military academies, both seem to have cultivated a sense of isolation, and both make extensive use of female children as beatific figures.

5. Klaus Karlstetter, "J. D. Salinger, R. W. Emerson and the Perennial Philosophy," *Moderna Sprak*, LXIII, 1969, 224–236.

6. Robert Lee Stuart, "The Writer-in-Waiting," *Christian Century*, 19 May 1965, pp. 647–649.

7. Bernice and Sanford Goldstein, "Bunnie and Cobras: Zen Enlightenment in Salinger," *Discourse*, XIII, Winter 1970, 98–106.

8. John Antico, "The Parody of J. D. Salinger: Esmé and the Fat Lady Exposed," *Modern Fiction Studies*, XII, Autumn 1966, 325–340.

9. John Updike, *New York Herald Tribune Book Review*, 17 September 1961, p. 27.

10. Alfred Kazin, *Atlantic*, Aug. 1961, p. 27.

11. *Time*, 15 September 1961, p. 84.

12. S. J. Rowland, *Christian Century*, 6 Oct. 1961, p. 1464.

13. A. E. Mayhew, *Commonweal*, 6 Oct. 1961, p. 48.

14. Granville Hicks, *Saturday Review*, 16 Sept. 1961, p. 26.

15. Irving Howe, *New York Times Book Review*, 7 April 1963, p. 4.

16. Ihab Hassan, "Almost the Voice of Silence: The Later Novelettes of J. D. Salinger," *Wisconsin Studies in Contemporary Literature*, IV, Winter 1963, 5–20.

17. Lyle Glazier, "The Glass Family Saga: Argument and Epiphany," *College English*, XXVII, Dec. 1965, 248–251.

18. Helen Weinberg, *The New Novel in America: The Kafkan Mode in Contemporary Fiction* (Ithaca: Cornell University Press, 1970), p. 147.

19. Alan W. Watts, *The Way of Zen* (New York, Pantheon, 1957), p. 174.

20. Howe, p. 4.

21. John Wain, *New Republic*, 16 Feb. 1963, p. 21.

22. Paul Levine, "J. D. Salinger: The Development of the Misfit Hero," in *J. D. Salinger and His Critics*, p. 114.

23. J. J. Quinn, *Best Sellers*, 1 Feb. 1963, p. 408.

24. Ihab Hassan, *Saturday Review*, 26 Jan. 1963, p. 38.

25. J. D. Salinger, "Hapworth 16, 1924," *The New Yorker*, XLI, 19 June 1965, 34.

26. Salinger, "Hapworth," p. 60.

27. Stanley Edgar Hyman, *Standards*, p. 27, cited by Max F. Schulz in "Epilogue to *Seymour: An Introduction*: Salinger and the Crisis of Consciousness," *Studies in Short Fiction*, V, 1968, 128.

RICHARD ALLAN DAVISON

Salinger Criticism and "The Laughing Man": A Case of Arrested Development

I

Published commentary on J. D. Salinger has slowed down considerably during the last fifteen years or so.[1] A kind of depression has followed that remarkable boom of the early sixties. Salinger himself has not published anything since *Hapworth 16, 1924* in the June 19, 1965 *New Yorker.*[2] His only public sign of life has been an irate response to the 1974 pirated edition of his previously uncollected short stories, and that was in a phone call to a San Francisco agent of *The New York Times.*[3] Despite his relative silence, however, the word is that he continues to write.[4] And so do a devoted number of Salinger's commentators, some of whom form the nucleus of a new generation of scholars and critics writing about an author who continues to command a very substantial audience.[5]

The scholars who have been working quietly during the lull following the plethora of activity produced by the Salinger Industry (the phrase is George Steiner's) went public in Chicago at a special Salinger session at the 1977 Modern Language Association convention which included three panelists who are working on book-length studies of Salinger: Dennis L. O'Connor (Georgetown University), James P. Doyle (Fordham University) and Eberhard Alsen (SUNY Cortland). Another member of the enthusiastic audience (enthusiastic at 8:30 A.M.!), Warren French, has recently revised a book so seminal to Salinger studies.[6] While Doyle's book will be a general

From *Studies in Short Fiction* 18, no. 1 (Winter 1981): 1–15. Copyright © 1981 by Newberry College.

introduction to Salinger's writing, O'Connor and Alsen are focusing on Salinger's use of Eastern thought[7] and its impact on our understanding of his later works. With "Teddy" (January 31, 1953) as a possible turning point in Salinger's career, as he allegedly moved from realism to (what was labeled at the Chicago session) a kind of neo-romanticism, their interests seem to be more with that later material signaled by the publication of this, the last of Salinger's *Nine Stories*. The later material includes, of course, *Franny* (1955), *Raise High the Roof Beam, Carpenters* (1965), *Zooey* (1957), *Seymour: An Introduction* (1959), and *Hapworth 16, 1924* (1985). In fact, there is talk of another special Modern Language Association session on Salinger, one devoted wholly to his last published work, the elusive and mind-boggling *Hapworth*. No doubt many more critics are lying back quietly waiting for Salinger's next publication. If a Salinger revival is in the offing, and it seems inevitable, it will have to go some to match the volume of output during the late fifties and early sixties. No post WWII writer was more discussed.

II

By 1962, however, Salinger criticism had peaked. The next year Louis D. Rubin asked "Why is it, one wonders, that the work of J. D. Salinger has attracted the critical attention of so many scholars?"[8] That same year Joseph Blotner voiced hopes " . . . for a moratorium on Salinger criticism. . . ."[9] In 1964 William T. Stafford saw even more reason for a respite: "Although studies continue to proliferate in Salinger, many of them are repetitious and unoriginal." He wondered " . . . how long this writing more about less and less in Salinger can continue."[10] Stafford devotes two and a half pages of his section in *American Literary Scholarship* (1965) to Salinger but mainly to praise James E. Miller's *J. D. Salinger* (University of Minnesota Pamphlets on American Writers, No. 51) of that same year. He rates Miller's book as " . . . quite possibly the best word yet written on the fiction of Salinger."[11] Yet while "The Salinger Industry rolls right along"[12] the quality of many of the products has declined. The 1966 *American Literary Scholarship Annual* still devotes a separate section to Salinger but it is only one page long. Disturbed by the inferior criticism, Stafford laments: "Other items on Salinger during the year are hardly better. . . ."[13] Richard D. Lehan, succeeding Stafford in the 1967 *Annual*, no longer giving Salinger a special section, lumps him with Robert Penn Warren under "Others" and announces that "The Salinger boom seems safely over if the year's scanty amount is any indication."[14] The 1968 *Annual* has James H. Justice returning to a (one page) special section for Salinger but echoing earlier uneasiness: "The year's work confirms an impression some have felt for several years: some day, after a decent interval, this erratic artist must be read with fresh premises and techniques which do not imitate Salinger's own."[15] In 1969 Salinger is all but lost in a section with Saul Bellow and Bernard Malamud. With one paragraph Justice dutifully notes the " . . . only two pieces on Salinger . . ."[16] And in 1970 Salinger is overwhelmed by Malamud, just as in 1971 Malamud and Bellow again all but squeeze him out. Justice's quote from French is anticlimactically appropriate: "Salinger's popularity has declined. . . ."[17] In 1972 Salinger is lumped once again with Bellow and Malamud and again given less space, barely two thirds of a page.[18] By 1973 Flannery O'Connor has her own four and a half page section while Salinger, now housed with Phillip Roth and I. B. Singer, is allotted two sentences.[19] Margaret Ann O'Connor takes over as reviewer in 1974 and dispatches Salinger in one short paragraph, discussing two articles.[20] Nor does she hint of a Salinger revival in the 1975 *Annual*.[21] What we have had, then, is a relative moratorium on Salinger commentary for almost a decade. It is time for some re-examinations and, if I read the signs rightly, it looks as if the Salinger and Eastern Thought Company will soon be selling stock.

III

At the risk of running counter to this gathering trend in Salinger scholarship and criticism, I will focus my own remarks on an earlier story, a story that seems to predate Salinger's obsession with Eastern Thought, a story that has been pretty much neglected. For even during the bullish days of the Salinger Industry "The Laughing Man" never received the attention it deserves. Unlike the vastly more popular "A Perfect Day for Bananafish" (January 31, 1948), "For Esmé—with Love and Squalor" (April 8, 1950), and "Teddy" (not to mention "Uncle Wiggily in Connecticut," "Just Before the War with the Eskimos," "Pretty Mouth and Green My Eyes," "Down at the Dinghy," and "De Daumier Smith's Blue Period"),[22] "The Laughing Man" does not have a single article devoted exclusively to it. I hope in this essay to fill some of that relative void and perhaps open a fresh discussion of Salinger's "realistic" short stories before they are buried in an avalanche of criticism on the so-called "neo-romantic" works.

To provide a clearer context for my discussion, a brief review of the rather sparse commentary on "The Laughing Man" is in order. One discovers that even the book-length studies of Salinger do not feature "The Laughing Man," although it is in Gwynn and Blotner and French that we find some of the most helpful (albeit brief) discussions of this story, which was first published in *The New Yorker* (March 19, 1949) and later became the fourth collected in *Nine Stories* (1952). Gwynn and Blotner open their two and a half page discussion with high praise: "Apparently simple, it turns out to be one of the most sophisticated and intricate of all Salinger's tales."[23] It is judged

" . . . a great improvement over its ridiculous and distant source, Victor Hugo's *L'Homme Qui Rit* (1869). . . ."[24] They correctly see Salinger's story as " . . . the recollection by a mature man of a crucial experience at the age of nine: the end of a hero-worship-laden relationship with an idealized older man . . . ;"[25] but they wholly ignore the agonizing problems of that "older man," the twenty-two or twenty-three-year-old law student and coach to twenty-five adolescent members of the Comanche Club. George Steiner in "The Salinger Industry" first calls "The Laughing Man" along with "Down at the Dinghy" " . . . fine sketches of the bruised, complicated world of children," but then adds that " . . . neither holds a candle to Joyce's 'Araby' or to the studies of childhood in Dostoevsky."[26] Adult implications are again all but ignored. William Wiegand claims that Salinger is seeking the remedy from banana fever (a central consideration of the adult-centered "A Perfect Day for Bananafish") in "The Laughing Man" through "sublimation in art."[27] Only in *Raise High the Roof Beam* is Salinger " . . . at last able to expose the banana fish. . . . Banana fever no longer seems the shame it did in 'Pretty Mouth,' 'The Laughing Man,' 'For Esmé,' and in 'Perfect Day' . . . itself . . ."[28] In "The Rare Quixotic Gesture" Ihab Hassan treats Gedsudski's story of the Laughing Man (a story within a story) astutely but summarily: "Here the story of the fabulous Laughing Man is itself a quixotic gesture which has the power to influence the youthful audience of the boys, including the narrator of Salinger's story, but is powerless to save Gedsudski."[29] Hassan doesn't explore why Gedsudski is not saved. Most of the remaining critics evidence either diminished concern with the story or a lessened ability to deal with it. This is certainly true of the essays gathered in the seven collections of Salinger criticism.

    Henry Anatole Grunwald's *Salinger, A Critical and Personal Portrait* contains no reference to "The Laughing Man" outside of the reprinted Steiner essay and the revised Hassan essay. William E. Belcher's and James W. Lee's 1962 *J. D. Salinger and the Critics* includes comments on some twenty[30] of Salinger's short stories (including seven[31] of the *Nine*) but not a word on "The Laughing Man."[32] In Harold P. Simonson's and Philip E. Hagen's 1963 *Salinger's Catcher in the Rye: Clamor vs Criticism,*[33] the numerous references to Salinger's stories do not include "The Laughing Man." It is mentioned only once in Malcolm Marsden's *If You Really Want To Know: A Catcher Casebook*[34] and then in another reprint of George Steiner's essay.[35] The only mention of "The Laughing Man" in the *Special Number: Salinger* (Winter, 1963) of *Wisconsin Studies in Contemporary Literature* is in Donald M. Fiene's bibliography. He notes that "The Laughing Man" was " . . . selected by Martha Foley as one of the distinguished short stories published in American magazines in 1949."[36] Nor do Marvin Laser and Norman Fruman, editing *Studies in J. D. Salinger: Reviews, Essays and Critiques* of *The Catcher in the Rye and Other*

Fiction that same year, add anything to our knowledge of "The Laughing Man."[37] Although there are articles in the last book-length study of Salinger, the *J. D. Salinger Special Number* of *Modern Fiction Studies* (Autumn 1968), dealing with "Esmé" and "Pretty Mouth" at length, "The Laughing Man" is mentioned only once, again in passing.[38]

The best and most extended (although just slightly longer than Gwynn's and Blotner's) discussion of "The Laughing Man" is still found in Warren French's *J. D. Salinger.*[39] He also spends more time on Gedsudski, referring to at least the suggestion of "adult pettiness," his willingness to "sacrifice children's feelings in order to salve his own wounds," and "the inner ruthlessness that motivates the self-made man" (p. 93). French feels, however, that Salinger fails in his portrayal of Gedsudski: "It is finally impossible to tell whether the intention is to exalt or expose Gedsudski" (p. 94). Most of French's focus is on the narrator. He argues that the story " . . . does not concern the romantic break-up [between John Gedsudski and Mary Hudson], but the effects of this break-up on the narrator: he suffers the double disillusionment of seeing the man he idolizes frustrated and of losing a source of innocent pleasure with the abrupt ending of the story about the Laughing Man" (pp. 92–93). French argues well, as far as he goes. If there is an error here it is in his over-emphasis on the narrator's emotional experience—his rite of passage.

IV

It has become almost a reflex action in this era of hypersensitive attention to the center of consciousness in literature to read any story told from the first person point of view as being mostly concerned with the spokesman and his self-revelations at the expense of the other characters—even if they be major characters in the story. Certainly Nick Caraway is almost as important as Jay Gatsby, and Jake Barnes is clearly more important than Robert Cohn, as both narrators reveal themselves in even the most minute of their observations. Perhaps it is time to pay more heed to the other main characters so crucial to the narrators' stories. Oliver Evans, for instance, may have been not so wrongheaded when he suggested that Ole Anderson may be the main protagonist in Hemingway's "The Killers" after all.[40] Perhaps the 1946 Burt Lancaster movie was not so fatuous in its greater emphasis on the despairing ex-fighter than on an incredulous Nick Adams.

This plea for a closer look beyond the first person narrator is particularly relevant to a closer scrutiny of Salinger's "The Laughing Man." Although the story, viewed through the center of consciousness of the unnamed nine-year-old and told from the hindsight of this boy as an adult (who is, incidentally, the same age as both Salinger and Buddy Glass were in 1949), does reveal much about his traumatic rite of passage, it is as much an examination of

John Gedsudski, Chief of the Comanche Club, and the reverberations of his
ill-fated love affair with Mary Hudson. Certainly "The Laughing Man" is
an account of a young boy's initiation into the painful complexities of adult
life as clearly as are such stories as Sherwood Anderson's "I Want To Know
Why," Hemingway's "My Old Man," and Robert Penn Warren's "Blackberry
Winter," but it is also a probing of the older Gedsudski's similar initiation. It
is a story of two neophytes (one a physical child, the other an emotional adolescent) who struggle in their initial encounters with the mysteries of sex and
adult responsibility. Gedsudski's own fictional creation, the Laughing Man,
is, in part, a metaphor for both struggles. Mary Hudson serves as a catalyst
for the simultaneous tests of both Gedsudski and his charge. She demands of
them a new involvement with which they are powerless to cope.

The worlds of the Comanches and their Chief (and that of the Laughing Man) appear under control and relatively untroubled until Mary's photograph appears above the rear-view mirror in Gedsudski's reconverted (and
ominously "condemned looking") bus. The male worlds have remained invio-
late (while in Gedsudski's story the bandit chief's mother is murdered and the
Laughing Man's Eurasian beauty endures unrequited love). Through her picture[41] Mary is associated with an instrument of measurement, taking "on the
unarresting personality of a speedometer." At first the photograph "clashed
with the men-only[42] décor of the bus" (p. 93). It is a puzzling complica-
tion in the boys' lives. Soon everything during their playtime hours becomes
geared to Mary's presence. Mary's picture increasingly insinuates itself into
the Comanche routine until Mary herself materializes. Gedsudski disrupts
the Comanche schedule (and violates his obligation to their parents), driving
one-half mile out of the way and holding up their baseball game to indulge
his selfish concern, his growing infatuation for Mary Hudson. Everything
becomes affected by her. Her very presence reveals in the erstwhile unflappa-
ble Chief "what had formerly been a well-concealed flair for incompetence."
She causes him to pull loose the gearshift knob and makes his usually expert
driving at best uncertain as the bus starts "with an amateurlike lurch" (p. 95).

Mary intrudes herself into the all-male passenger bus just as she later
intrudes herself into the Comanches' baseball game. The boys, at first hostile,
come to accept her, but only after she proves able to meet them on their
own terms, at bat[43] on the ballfield. She meets Gedsudski on his own play-
ground, as it were, literally and figuratively. Gedsudski is ecstatic when she
hits a triple, handling the bat with surprising control. It seems, at the time,
that by blending in with boyish activities she will not disturb his cloistered
adolescent world after all. But too much, apparently, has transpired behind
the scenes. Her actions remain enigmatic. Seeming at once aggressive and
hesitant, she always goes past first base but is never described as reaching

home plate. Salinger, in fact, most often associates her with third base, forever in scoring position but never scoring. She waves at the narrator from there: "She happened to be a girl who knew how to wave to somebody from third base" (p. 98). Her final argument with Gedsudski takes place there, and it is from near third base that she bids her final tearful goodbye. Their worlds are to remain apart.

Mary's character, as Salinger presents it, is an ambivalent one. She seems both the epitome of a spoiled rich brat out of a Fitzgerald[44] story and a loving woman who looks for a man and finds instead a slightly overgrown boy scout. It may be that she rejects Gedsudski's attentions just as she rejects the narrator's overtures to her tears. But it is also clear that neither male is prepared to respond with maturity. The narrator admits he did not understand her tears.[45] Gedsudski lets her run from the ball field. He is not willing to go far enough out of his way to repair their shattered relationship. Salinger further associates Mary with baby carriages, reinforcing her separation from (or closeness to!) Gedsudski and the boy. (One is tempted to trot out the old schoolboy chant: "First comes love, then comes marriage, then comes Gedsudski with a baby carriage," epitomizing his 'aw shucks' adolescent attitude toward matrimony and offspring.) On that last day we see Mary sitting on a bench between two baby carriages.[46] Gedsudski walks over to her and brings her to his game area. After they argue and Gedsudski elects not to follow as she makes her final exit, the puzzled narrator trips over a baby carriage on his way to the bus. Salinger's juxtaposition of the boy's physical obstacle with the man's emotional one is overt. Just as it is never clear that the breakup is Mary's fault, so there is reason to believe that male inadequacy is at least a contributing factor to it.

Throughout the story both the boy and Gedsudski seem to have an adolescent fear of and/or naiveté toward sex and its adult associations. If Gedsudski is balking at such adult responsibility (which, at least in 1928 and 1949, traditionally led to marriage), the boy seems fatefully tuned to his chief's emotional vibrations. Gedsudski's apparent reluctance to leave his boyhood environment and fulfill his role as lover/father provokes Mary's tears and alienation more than do their social class differences. This break between the sophisticated young Wellesley graduate with "her Herbert Tareyton cigarettes (cork tipped)" and her beaver coat and the young socially and emotionally retarded first- or second-year law student seems inevitable. Salinger has carefully prepared us for Gedsudski's inability to communicate with the adult world. Rather than being confused about Gedsudski (as others have suggested) Salinger presents him brilliantly in all of his complexities within a world that shares the complexities of its protagonist. The narrator's own feelings[47] about the Chief may be as ambivalent as Holden's are about D.B. and the movies. But the Gedsudski he remembers never comes to positive terms with himself or his world. The creature of Gedsudski's imagination fares no better. The Comanche Chief and the Laughing Man share similar inhibitions. They are also the role models for twenty-five boys.

V

Gedsudski's complex character is more subtly explored in the interior narrative. Rather than send the reader into a Chinese box succession of reality levels as Albee does in *Tiny Alice*, or into an endless succession of stories within stories as Barth does in "Menelaiad," Salinger establishes more of a one-to-one relationship between John Gedsudski and the Laughing Man. Not merely a wish fulfillment, Gedsudski's creation is a metaphor for the teller's own special vulnerabilities and defenses and for their ultimate failure. The Laughing Man, with his sexual inhibitions and pseudo-Christian overtones[48] (complete with crucifixion), is a more grotesque counterpart of his creator. Although the imaginative creation of the Laughing Man is in *part* wish fulfillment, Gedsudski's own big-nosed, low-browed squat figure is scarcely compensated for by the noseless,[49] flatheaded, skinny counterpart. This creation is scarcely a physical improvement. He must try to offset even greater handicaps. For Gedsudski's Laughing Man is not so much an escape from his own ugliness, his own sense of immaturity, as an exaggeration of these things. Through the Laughing Man he can plunge more deeply into grotesque disfigurement and alienation only to rise higher in vicarious triumph. It is Gedsudski's way of proving to himself and the Comanches that even a being beyond the limits of acceptable appearance and mature human communion, someone, in other words, immeasurably worse off than Gedsudski, can still command awe, respect and love. The Laughing Man is a logical hero for Gedsudski to create. Like an adolescent fantasy incarnate, the Laughing Man must maintain the invincibility of a Superman who is capable of merciless revenge on those who flout the rules of fair play. But anyone with such a selfish demand for a personal kind of poetic justice is also vulnerable and may crumple like his comic strip counterpart when yesterday's newspaper is discarded.

Both Gedsudski and the Laughing Man have attempted to overcome their ugliness by either a superior ability at sports or a masterful ability to accumulate a fortune, by showing off the "unclassifiably" beautiful Mary Hudson or continually outwitting the "internationally famous" DuFarges. While Gedsudski is more overtly athletic, the Laughing Man, who is "as graceful as a cat on his feet" (p. 88), sports "an underground gymnasium and a shooting range" (p. 91) beneath his tiny cottage. Gedsudski's sportsmanship is reflected in the Laughing Man's "singular love of fairplay" (p. 89). Gedsudski thrives

on the admiration of the Comanches who see in him a smooth amalgama-
tion of "the most photogenic features of Buck Jones, Ken Maynard and Tom
Mix ..." (p. 88). The Laughing Man, shunned by most humans, befriends
all "species of animals" and is adored by four "blindly loyal confederates" (p.
91). "They [do] not think him ugly" (p. 88). He shares with Gedsudski a
pleasant voice and speaks to his animals "in their own tongues" (p. 88) as
effectively as Gedsudski communicates with his children. Clearly the Chief
needs his Comanches, perhaps more than the Laughing Man needs Omba,
the dwarf, and his other loyal followers. Downfall in both men involves alienation from their followers. Ultimately Gedsudski's loss of control, beginning
with his bad driving, continuing with his swearing and ending with the ego-
shattering breakup with Mary, is more nobly reflected in the Laughing Man's
final encounter with the DuFarges when, hoping that he can save his beloved
timber wolf, Black Wing, he allows himself to be fatally outwitted by these
arch enemies.

Both Gedsudski's revenge and the Laughing Man's sacrificial death
serve to externalize the boys' reactions to parental neglect or indifference. The
Laughing Man himself may be symbolically repudiating his own orphan-
age upbringing as he sets up the death of the bandit chief's mother.[50] The
Comanches' own home environments exude parental rejection. Have the
young boys' parents rejected them as the society in Gedsudski's story has
rejected the Laughing Man? If not, why do the boys' parents farm them out
every day after school and all day on Saturdays and holidays? Why does each
boy see himself as the only real ("legitimate") son of the Laughing Man, dis-
avowing his "bogus" parents? Do not the narrator's parents show insensitivity
when they send their traumatized child to bed uncomforted? In revising the
concluding sentence of the *New Yorker* version of "The Laughing Man" for
Nine Stories, Salinger placed more onus on the parents by pointing up the
absence of any physical contact with the boy. (Compare "I arrived home with
my teeth chattering uncontrollably and had to be put to bed" with the more
impersonal "I arrived home with my teeth chattering uncontrollably and was
told to go right straight to bed.") They seem to be treating an emotional
trauma as they would a common chill.

The ability to endure rejection and transcend it is, of course, central to
the maturation process. One must cope with rejection and grow because of
and/or in spite of the experience. All three main characters are stunned by
their encounters and are swallowed up by the resulting void. Unlike Holden
Caulfield, they do not allow a Phoebe to ignite their lives with a spark of
salvation. While the boy passively accepts the temporary security of his bed,
Gedsudski and the Laughing Man actively resist redemption, for acceptance
of help involves commitment and obligation. Acceptance of responsibility

involves more maturity than they have attained. The physical ugliness of both creator and creation externalizes this absence of mature sexual responsibility that permeates both Gedsudski's real world and his fantasy world.

The fantastic exploits of the Laughing Man reveal the intensity of Gedsudski's attempts to remain impregnable in his tenuous role as hero-counselor-umpire-guide to the Comanches. In his subconscious Gedsudski may be more sensitive to those liabilities exaggerated by the social gap between Mary Hudson (Wellesley, Early American Heritage, Upper Class, Long Island) and himself (New York University, Second Generation American, Lower Class, Staten Island) than Mary is. He tries in vain to close this gap by creating in his fictional serial the distant-closeness of the Chinese-Paris border. In Gedsudski's story, we recall, it is the Eurasian girl—not the Laughing Man—who suffers from unrequited love. He shows her little charity. In fact, Hoang, the giant, and the girl are further from the Laughing Man's favors than the weaker dwarf and the non-human wolf. Those he can most easily dominate pose a lesser challenge to the insularity of his existence. The whole Laughing Man fantasy iterates Gedsudski's need to remain a professional companion of boys, to remain in their eyes an "impartial and unexcitable umpire at all [their] bedlam sporting events, . . . master fire builder and extinguisher, and . . . expert, uncontemptuous first-aid man" (p. 85).

Every detail in Salinger's description of his storyteller's background and accomplishments seems calculated to emphasize Gedsudski's success at boyish games in a boyish world. He is never shown successful in a single adult endeavor. Gedsudski is an Eagle scout and exudes the youthful tenacity required to pile up dutifully the prerequisite merit badges (including fire building and first aid). Salinger notes that he was *invited* to the New York Giants baseball camp; there is no evidence that he successfully attended it. He seems to have made no attempt to compete with adults even within the context of his boyhood game. Salinger further notes that he was *almost* All-American tackle. His status at law school is not explored but his tenure is during a time (1928) when most students were neither renowned for their protests nor for their sophisticated involvement in adult activities. In any case, that part of his life remains unexplored.

Perhaps there is more than a hint here of a Salinger parody of society's blind worship of the college athlete-hero who is so often a part of the Horatio Alger American success story. F. Scott Fitzgerald (who clearly influenced Salinger) was capable of this kind of semi-parody in such stories as "The Freshest Boy," where Basil Duke Lee's "acceptance" by his peers is tinged with irony. At times the portrait of Mary Hudson is reminiscent of those apparently unattainable society girls sought by the Dexter Greens and Gatsbys and scorned by the Anson Hunters. Salinger also may be disclosing Gedsudski's blind adherence to an image of an unattainable girl who may be in reality a warm and responsive woman.

In any case Salinger consistently portrays Gedsudski as balking at adult commitment and suggests his emotional inability to fulfill the role of lover/ husband. Gedsudski's refusal to leave the world of children is not unlike Holden's treasuring of childhood innocence and Seymour's attempts to find solace in his communication with the four-year-old Sybil. While Holden strives to resolve his distrust of the adult world by talking to the reader and Seymour dodges into suicide, Gedsudski murders the creature of his imagination, his alter ego. The Laughing Man ultimately has proved as useless in his life struggle as (in "Uncle Wiggily in Connecticut") Jimmy Jimmereeno is to Ramona's.[51] Gedsudski's adolescent hesitation is, of course, no cure for Mary's tears and the subsequent alienation. He engages in what is a symbolic suicide and murder, a murder not only of the Laughing Man but also of the dreams of twenty-five children. That Mary comes near the Chief's territory on that last day may suggest on her part an attempt at reconciliation. Perhaps the narrator's dinner invitation to Mary is an intuitive attempt to compensate for a felt deficiency in his chief. (Or is the invitation the result of an unconscious rivalry prompted by a schoolboy crush of his own?) The boy experiences physically and emotionally (if not intellectually) the agony his chief is enduring but not controlling. After Gedsudski's traumatic parting with Mary climaxes in the death of the Laughing Man, the narrator's teeth chatter "uncontrollably" from his own sense of rejection. The appearance of a facsimile of the Laughing Man's poppy mask exacerbates the boy's emotional upheaval by extending the fictional account beyond the world of fantasy. The "tissue paper" reminder is doubly painful because of its association with the Laughing Man. For to the boy at this moment Gedsudski's creation has become a greater object of sympathy[52] than Gedsudski himself. Certainly to the reader Gedsudski's callous masochistic and/or sadistic murder of the Laughing Man suggests the self-centered peevishness of a child who has not gotten what he may (or may not) have truly wanted.

While the reader is touched by, delights in and then mourns the Laughing Man, he comes gradually to harbor uneasy and uncertain feelings about Gedsudski. The early hints of Gedsudski's failure at adult activities, carrying with it a latent cruelty, serve as a matrix for the ill success in his love affair. As soon as Mary's presence is evident to the Comanches, they also witness in their Chief the beginning of what is to them his transformation, his loss of control. On the day of the final encounter with Mary his wet-combed hair and substitution of an adult's overcoat for a boyish leather windbreaker continue to reflect a superficial and futile attempt to camouflage a deeper absence of mature commitment. The mere doffing of a windbreaker for an overcoat proves no impediment to his ultimate retreat into childish petulance. Gedsudski may emerge from his trials sadder and more aware of adult complexities, but even the ritualistic murder of the Laughing Man which extends beyond the world of imagination does not ensure his putting away all adolescent things. At the end of the story he may be both embittered and relieved: the reader imagines him sitting alone in his emptied bus after the Comanches have stepped out into their far less certain world. That the nine-year-old narrator seems more profoundly affected than his chief pointedly underscores Gedsudski's state of arrested development.

VI

It is a truism that Salinger deals most frequently with the misfit or outsider in society. It is also true that he has become well known largely as a writer about exceptional children. Yet some of his most perceptive revelations (especially in *Nine Stories*) concern either adults or those on the verge of adulthood. "The Laughing Man" is one of many stories that offer more acute insights on adults than on children. Holden, as narrator, is seventeen; Franny and De Daumier Smith are both nineteen. Zooey, Buddy and Seymour are viewed most frequently as adults. "A Perfect Day for Bananafish" centers on Muriel and Seymour: "For Esmé with Love and Squalor" focuses on Sergeant X, not the children, and "Down at the Dinghy" is as much or more about a sensitive mother's understanding of her child than it is about the four-year-old runaway. "Just Before the War with the Eskimos" concerns a teenager and a twenty-four-year-old misfit, while "Uncle Wiggily in Connecticut" deals more with the self-absorbed mother than her ill-adjusted daughter. "Pretty Mouth and Green My Eyes" is wholly about adults and the artificiality, sterility, cruelty and pathos in adult relationships. Even "Teddy," which does focus on a ten-year-old, relies heavily on the adult reactions of, notably, the McArdles and Nicolson for a complete portrait of this boy genius. Perhaps Salinger should be viewed as a writer about adults and his canon re-examined in this light.

As he got more concerned with Eastern thought he seems to have translated his views into fiction that increasingly reflects the Mahayana, Zen and Vedanta philosophies. Yet before one can fully comprehend what Salinger is doing in the later works it is crucial to re-examine his concerns in the earlier ones. His preoccupation then, I submit, is largely with adult considerations and adult struggles in which all of the actions of children are judged against a norm that, when not of Christ, is of an adult world with its flaws and imperfections, its phoniness and cruelty, but a world also peopled with the D.B.'s and the Mr. Antolinis, whose hearts may have lost some of the purity but none of the love. If the Gedsudskis of this world do not radiate ultimately positive values, it is because they are doomed to reside in a perennially arrested state where values are not so much childlike as childish.

Afterword upon Reading the Article in 2011

Many of Salinger's stories clearly deal with rites of passage, the often painful struggle to put away (or avoid putting away) childish things. Salinger knew of "the fortunate fall" and could have had Gedsudski deliberately kill the Laughing Man to shock his neophytes out of their dependence on childhood fantasies to better prepare them for the hardships of adulthood.

But if such an intent is inherent in "The Laughing Man," it is Salinger's, not Gedsudski's. For Gedsudski remains too wrapped up in his emotional reaction to whatever prompted Mary to run away from him. His treatment of the boys on the bus still seems self-centered and meanspirited. The hero caretaker turned bully takes out his hurt, his misplaced aggression on his nine-year-old dependents. Although I may sympathize with Gedsudski more than I did more than thirty years ago, Salinger's chief remains a vulnerable victim of his immaturity rather than a would-be protector/savior of twenty-five children.

NOTES

1. There is only one article on Salinger noted by Margaret Anne O'Connor in *American Literary Scholarship: an Annual/1975* (Durham: Duke University Press, 1977). Hans Galinsky cites one from a German festschrift and Keiko Beppu has discovered an essay from Japan. This is a far cry from the peak years of Salinger criticism. . . .

2. Magazine copies of this story, which features an incredibly precocious seven-year-old Seymour, are becoming rarer each year. Many library copies have been stolen or mutilated.

3. For an account of Salinger's comments see Lacey Fosburg's "J. D. Salinger Speaks About His Silence," *New York Times*, November 3, 1974, pp. 1, 89.

4. Brendan Gill, for instance, assures us that Salinger is still hard at work. See *Here At the New Yorker* (New York: Random House, 1975), p. 226.

5. Sales of his paperbacks continue to move briskly. College students remain enthusiastic about both *Catcher in the Rye* and *Nine Stories*.

6. *J. D. Salinger*, Twayne's United States Authors Series, No. 40 (New York: Twayne Publishers Inc.; 1968; rpt. Boston: G. K. Hall and Co., 1978).

7. Salinger's interest in the philosophy of the New and Old Testament, Advaita Vedanta and Classical Taoism as well as Mahayana and Zen literature was discussed most recently by Alsen and O'Connor at the 1977 Modern Language Association meeting.

8. *American Literary Scholarship: an Annual/1963* (Durham: Duke University Press, 1965), p. 148. Hereafter cited as *ALS* with the appropriate date.

9. *ALS* 1963, p. 147.

10. *ALS* 1964, p. 165.

11. *ALS* 1965, p. 193.

12. *ALS* 1965, p. 195.

13. *ALS* 1980, p. 180.

14. *ALS* 1967, p. 208.

15. *ALS* 1968, p. 219.

16. *ALS* 1969, p. 248.

17. See *ALS* 1970, pp. 281–282 and *ALS* 1971, p. 255 respectively.

18. *ALS* 1972, pp. 288–284.

19. *ALS* 1973, p. 278.

20. *ALS* 1974, pp. 281–282.

21. *ALS* 1975. See above.

22. These last five stories were also first published in magazines before being collected in *Nine Stories* (Boston: Little, Brown and Company, 1958). All page references will be to this edition. They appeared on the following respective dates: March 20, 1948 (*New Yorker*); June 5, 1948 (*New Yorker*); July 14, 1951 (*New Yorker*); April 1949 (*Harper's*); and May 1952 (*World Review*).

23. Frederick L. Gwynn and Joseph L. Blotner, *The Fiction of J. D. Salinger* (Pittsburgh: University of Pittsburgh Press, 1958), p. 24.

24. Gwynn and Blotner, p. 25.

25. Gwynn and Blotner, p. 24.

26. *The Nation*, 189 (November 14, 1959), 381.

27. "J. D. Salinger: Seventy-Eight Bananas," *Chicago Review*, 11 (Winter 1958), 10.

28. Wiegand, p. 15.

29. Henry Anatole Grunwald, ed. *Salinger: A Critical and Personal Portrait* (New York: Harper, 1982), p. 148. The original version of Hassan's essay ("Rare Quixotic Gesture: The Fiction of J. D. Salinger," *The Western Review*, 21 [Summer 1957], 281–280.) does not contain this reference.

30. There are some twenty short stories in various magazines that Salinger has chosen not to republish.

31. "Just Before the War With the Eskimos" is also omitted.

32. Belcher and Lee do reprint comments on "Bananafish" and "Esmé" from Gwynn and Blotner's *The Fiction of J. D. Salinger*.

33. Simonson and Hagen edited this collection (Boston: D. C. Heath and Co., 1963).

34. Marsden served as editor of this casebook (Chicago: Scotts, Foresman and Co., 1988).

35. See above.

36. Carl F. Strauch is the Advisory Editor for this Volume 4, Number 1 issue of *Wisconsin Studies in Contemporary Literature*.

37. The Laser and Fruman book was published by Odyssey Press in New York.

38. The Autumn 1968 issue of *Modern Fiction Studies* is Volume 12, Number 3. In 1965 James E. Miller, Jr. gave a once-over-lightly treatment of "The Laughing Man" along with "Dinghy," "Eskimos," "Wiggily," and "Pretty Mouth," while "Esmé" "De Daumier" "Teddy" and "Bananafish" are dealt with at greater length. See *J. D. Salinger*, University of Minnesota Pamphlets on American Writers. Minneapolis, 1965.

39. French, pp. 91–94. See above.

40. See Oliver Evans' "The Protagonist of Hemingway's 'The Killers,'" *Modern Language Notes*, 12 (December 1958), 589–591.

41. Mary Hudson is shown "dressed in academic cap and gown" (p. 93), a constant reminder of her graduation from undergraduate life.

42. Although in 1928 as well as 1949 clubs were typically segregated by sex, Salinger seems to be underlining the exclusively male existence of Gedsudski and the Comanches.

43. No doubt there may be conscious Freudian implications on Salinger's part concerning her expert handling of the bat: "[Gedsudski] told her not to choke the bat too tightly. 'I'm not,' she said" (p. 98). Mary Hudson remains a precarious outfielder, however, as she is as ineffectual on fly balls as Holden Caulfield is in his attempts to prevent the children of his world from plunging off the cliff at the edge of the field of rye.

44. Among the possible echoes of Fitzgerald are those from "The Diamond as Big As The Ritz." Like Braddock Washington The Laughing Man amasses "the largest personal fortune in the world" (p. 90). While Washington converts his diamonds into radium and places it into bank vaults, The Laughing Man converts his "fortune into diamonds and lowers it into emerald vaults . . ." (pp. 90–91). Washington puts his potential enemies in a huge glass bowl in the earth. The Laughing Man incarcerates his in a "deep but pleasantly decorated mausoleum" (p. 89).

45. In the book version Salinger allows the narrator a glimmer of understanding. The parenthetical statement in the magazine version: "I had no idea what was going on between the Chief and Mary Hudson (and still haven't). . . ." (p. 31) is changed to "(and still haven't, in any but a fairly low, intuitive sense) . . ." (p. 105).

46. Salinger initiates the baby carriage motif in this second paragraph of the story: "If we had straight athletics on our minds, we went . . . where the opposing team didn't include a baby carriage or an irate old lady with a cane." Freudian critics would see serially threatening implications in the "irate old lady with a cane." One could also argue (shades of the controversy in *Frannie*) that through the later association of Mary with "nursemaids with baby carriages" (p. 108) Salinger is implying that she is pregnant. Even the hint of such a condition is potential support for my argument concerning Gedsudski's fear of adult responsibility.

47. Although the question of the narrator's reliability is a difficult one, we must assume a certain objectivity on his part, even though, like Whitman's narrator in "Out of the Cradle Endlessly Rocking" ("A man, yet by these tears a little boy again"), he is moved as he relives the emotions of his childhood.

48. Salinger remarks early on his "singular love of fair play" (p. 89) and his "compassionate side" (p. 89). The Laughing Man remains chaste and befriends the lowly. He allows his enemy "to tie him with barbed wire to a tree" (p. 101) and suffers and dies there refusing "the vial of eagle's blood . . ." and giving up a " . . . heart-rending gasp of final sorrow . . ." (p. 110) at his death.

49. Noselessness has been associated quite frequently with lack of virility or impotence. See Rabelais and Sterne.

50. The hypocrisy of the Laughing Man's parents, a "wealthy missionary couple," is apparent when they refuse "(from a religious conviction) to pay the ransom for their son." The refusal prompts the bandits to place "the little fellow's head in a carpenter's vice," which leads, of course, to his hideous disfigurement (p. 87).

51. Ramona's pathetic attempt to replace the imaginative Jimmy Jimmereeno (whom she has run over by a car) with the equally unreal Mickey Mickeranno is another escape device no more successful than her mother's attempt to escape the sterile present through memories of the dead Walt Glass.

52. Certainly the gentleness the Laughing Man exhibits to his friends at his death is in sharp contrast to Gedsudski's cruelty to the boys. Even though their club is named after an Indian tribe noted for its bravery, there is no evidence to suggest he is merely testing them. Nor is there reason to believe that a comic point of the story may be in the fact that the teller sees the plight of Gedsudski as more tragic than it is, thus revealing his own immaturity.

JOHN WENKE

Sergeant X, Esmé, and the Meaning of Words

She went on to say that she wanted *all* her children to absorb the *meaning* of the words they sang, not just *mouth* them, like silly-billy parrots.

During a time when many writers are reconsidered, reconstructed, redis-covered, or revisited, the last ten years have been remarkable for the appar-ent decline of critical interest in J. D. Salinger. Over the last two decades, Salinger has had so little to say that his commentators, once a spirited and argumentative group, seem to have followed the lead of the master and have become, for the most part, silent. Many readers of Salinger's work vacillate regularly between the conviction that he is in New Hampshire composing masterpiece after masterpiece but refusing to publish, and the less fantastic, more sobering suspicion that he is simply growing vegetables and repeat-ing the Jesus prayer. Nevertheless, the small body of fiction remains as a cryptic reminder of a significant contemporary writer who has adopted an enigmatic public silence. While any resolution to the mystery of Salinger's silence must remain elusive for the moment, certain implications in his best short story may go some way in accounting for the retreat, without having to construe it as an outgrowth of his later preoccupation with Zen. His con-tinuing silence may well have evolved from the conviction that deeply-felt human emotions need no expression—a position implied by the successful aesthetic resolution of "For Esmé—with Love and Squalor."

From *Studies in Short Fiction* 18, no. 3 (Summer 1981): 251–59. Copyright © 1981 by Newberry College.

In the fifties and sixties, the critical debate over "For Esmé" focused on various aspects of love and squalor as they relate to the narrator (Sergeant X), Esmé, Charles, and Clay (Corporal Z).[1] While the story does in fact dramatize Sergeant X's redemption from an emotion and physical breakdown through the transformative powers of love, the narrative also—and most importantly—examines the reasons why forms of expression—whether conversational, literary, or epistolary, to name a few—either have meaning and propagate love, or lack meaning and impede emotional stability. For Salinger, failures of language advance the horror, vacuity, and despair of modern life. Throughout the narrative, Salinger reflects his concern with exploring the validity of language by persistently alluding to such indirect, constructed modes of discourse as letters, books, or inscriptions. Failed forms of communication seem to be everywhere, the most notable of which is Sergeant X's illegible response to a Nazi woman's inscription, "Dear God, life is hell," in Goebbels' "Die Zeit Ohne Beispiel." In "For Esmé" letters, books, conversations, and inscriptions usually create (or continue) rather than alleviate the emotional vacuum in which most of the characters live. Nowhere else in Salinger's fiction does he more intensely present the paradox and dilemma of modern man: to speak is not to express; to employ forms of expression is often to evade the difficulties of significant communication. Beneath the most obvious progression of action and theme in "For Esmé" resides the moral basis for Salinger's art which indicates why, at the end of the story, two successful acts of communication are completed, while, throughout most of the story itself, dramatizing the reasons why most acts of expression fail.

In a story replete with failed forms of communication, one must consider why Esmé's saving letter has such a positive effect, and how it has anything to do with the rest of the narrative as well as Salinger's later and continuing silence. These issues can be explored by first examining the story's many human relationships. In "For Esmé," it is difficult to find many instances of love based on sympathetic understanding and shared experiences. Debased, destructive relationships predominate and are manifested most vividly through the narrator's relation to his wife and mother-in-law, his fellow soldiers in camp, and Clay and Loretta. Underlying these failures of love and sympathy reside the breakdown and deterioration of the power of language to express true feeling.

At the outset of the story, Salinger satirizes the mundane actualities and practical considerations of post-war America. The narrator's wife, a "breathtakingly levelheaded girl," and the impending visit of Mother Grencher, who, at fifty-eight, is "not getting any younger," detain him from going to Esmé's wedding.[2] Apparently, the wife has little sense of Esmé's importance to her husband, and the narrator, while wryly undercutting his wife's practicality, does not seem capable of acting against her wishes. His tongue seems to be firmly in cheek as he ticks off the reasons why the proposed trip need not be made. In fact, he seems to be repeating the strictures as they were dictated to him. Such a failure marks a continuation of the "stale letters" the narrator received during the war. Reports on the service at Schrafft's and requests for cashmere yarn, like the prohibition against attending the wedding, extend selfish interests, while, at the same time, they evidence little concern for the narrator's needs.

His difficulties with these two women signal a problem that appears elsewhere in other forms—the sterility of conventional relationships. There is, for example, no fellowship among the troops at the training camp. The absence of community is predicated upon the failure of language. These letter-writing types, living in a self-imposed limbo, pen their letters in order to avoid human contact. The narrator, in particular, uses forms of expression to distance himself from those around him; he escapes, for example, into the books which he carries about in his gas mask container. His general disgust with experience appears most clearly through his use of cliché. Such tired language mocks the traditional bravado associated with war, and it exploits the disparity between fresh rhetorical assessments and degraded, sterile statements:

> I remember standing at an end window of our Quonset hut for a very long time, looking out at the slanting, dreary rain, my trigger finger itching imperceptibly, if at all. I could hear behind my back the uncomradely scratching of many fountain pens on many sheets of V-mail paper. Abruptly, with nothing special in mind, I came away from the window and put on my raincoat, cashmere muffler, galoshes, woolen gloves, and overseas cap. . . . Then, after synchronizing my wristwatch with the clock in the latrine, I walked down the long, wet cobblestone hill into town. I ignored the flashes of lightning all around me. They either had your number on them or they didn't. (pp. 88–89)

Just as the narrator's exploitation of cliché reflects the general bleakness of military life, so also does the perversion of romantic language point to significant failures in conventional ways of ordering experience. The relationship between Clay and Loretta is maintained through meaningless forms which make their courtship an exercise in mutual self-delusion. Intending to marry "at their earliest convenience," she writes to him "fairly regularly, from a paradise of triple exclamation points and inaccurate observations" (p. 108). Their relationship epitomizes the way in which language in "For Esmé" fails to communicate deep feeling, but instead propagates the antithesis of love—squalor. Salinger implies that their lack of self-awareness and moral introspection is not merely contemptible, but is actually a succinct embodiment of those very forces of insensitivity and self-justification which create and sustain the absurdity of war. Clay revels in the delusion that temporary insanity, rather than sadism, made him shoot a cat.

In "For Esmé—with Love and Squalor," such characters as the narrator's wife and mother-in-law, Clay and Loretta, are impervious to the existential ravage inflicted by the war; others, like the soldiers in the camp and the narrator himself, perceive the bleakness of experience but can do little or nothing to overcome it or escape from it. By escaping into letter-writing, into books, or by adopting a cynical attitude, they repudiate the possibility of community and compound their isolation through acts of quiet desperation.

Nonetheless, the very fact that the story is even told in the first place suggests that there is a way to be immersed in squalor, recognize it as such, and eventually overcome it. "For Esmé" depicts extreme human misery, the suffering of being unable to love, at the same time that the narrator's very capacity to tell his story provides the completion of the psychological therapy which began when he read Esmé's letter and fell asleep. In telling the story, the narrator has clearly achieved a balance in his life, which, at the outset of the story, is implied by his good-natured, if ironic, tone. Unlike all other attempts to communicate, Esmé's letter and the process of telling the tale itself come directly out of the forces underlying their personal encounter in the Devon tearoom and possess a basis in love which is founded upon similar recognitions of the effect of squalor on the other. These acts of communication are not spontaneous emanations, but come out of periods of retrospection and consolidation during which each perceives the import of that "strangely emotional" time which they spent together. Esmé's decision to send X her father's watch could not have been hasty or gratuitous. A six year period of recovery precedes the composition of the narrator's "squalid and moving" story. For Salinger, it seems, meaningful human expression must be founded on authentic emotions which evolve into a sympathetic comprehension of another's individual needs. Forms of expression are, in themselves, neutral; they become meaningful or parodic to the extent that love or squalor resides at the heart of the relationship. The love that Salinger affirms in "For Esmé" does not depend on words, but on an emotional inner transformation which must be understood and assimilated before it can be expressed. Forms of expression cannot create love, as Clay and Loretta try to do through letters, but only express what has mysteriously been there from the start. In "For Esmé," we encounter a significant moment in Salinger's fiction, a moment during which ineffable emotional states find expression in literary forms.

Given what has been argued thus far, it would he helpful to examine just how the conversation between the narrator and Esmé in the tearoom relates to his epiphany at the conclusion of the story. Basically, we shall see how their conversation offers vital insights into the psychological needs of each character, even though the apparent surface meaning of their words does not seem to indicate the formation of a deep and lasting bond of love.

For both the narrator and Esmé, language does not directly mirror their true inner states, but instead provides a defense, a kind of mask from behind which the suffering self cryptically speaks. The narrator adopts a protective cynicism, which largely accounts for the strange shiftings of tone and point of view evident throughout the meeting. Esmé's famous malaprops and inflated diction are the basic elements with which she constructs her persona. For both characters, language offers a way to cover-up their psychological fragility, insecurity, and acute self-consciousness, even though some very minor actions help to reflect most clearly the tenuousness of their respective poses. The narrator, for example, smiles but is careful to hide his "coalblack filling," while Esmé's fingernails are bitten to the quick and her tendency to keep touching her hair belies her posture of self-assurance.

It is probably not necessary to detail Esmé's strained attempts to appear older, more mature, self-possessed. Nonetheless, a brief look at the way the narrative voice oscillates between sarcasm and sincerity will suggest how language covers-up, rather than directly reflects, the true state of the narrator's being. When watching the choir practice, the narrator emanates a glib, sardonic attitude: "Their voices were melodious and unsentimental, almost to the point where a somewhat more denominational man than myself might, without straining, have experienced levitation" (p. 90). His deflation of the choir is offset a few lines later by a genuine admiration for Esmé's voice: "Her voice was distinctly separate from the other children's voices, and not just because she was seated nearest me. It had the best upper register, the sweetest-sounding, the surest, and it automatically led the way" (p. 90). During their conversation itself, his tone and emotional state continue to fluctuate between sarcasm and sincerity. When asked whether he attends that "secret Intelligence school on the hill," he notes that he is "as security-minded as the next one" and therefore tells Esmé that he is "visiting Devonshire for my health" (p. 94). Shortly thereafter, the narrator admits that he is glad she came over, since he "*had* been feeling lonely" (p. 95).

Generally, their conversation is amiable, congenial, interesting, and leaves the narrator pondering the "strangely emotional" moment which the departure of Charles and Esmé creates. On the surface, this meeting does not seem to satisfactorily explain Esmé's capacity to overwhelm X with love at the end of the story. On the basis of the language and action alone, one may be inclined to view Leslie Fiedler's nearly blasphemous assertion that "For Esmé" is "a popular little tearjerker" with some sympathy. The conversation, however, helps to suggest some basic facts about each character: the narrator is greatly in need of emotional sustenance; Esmé, midway between childhood and adulthood, must cope with the pain of having lost both parents at the same time that she must bear the responsibility of taking care of her brother. Their conversation implies, but does not explicitly record, the extent of each character's emotional reaction. Ultimately, one must perceive that, underlying the words and actions of this scene, some kind of inscrutable magnetism touches the narrator and Esmé, which evolves from an instinctual and unconscious sense that each possesses what the other most deeply needs. In light of the subsequent action, it can be argued that Esmé senses in the narrator the capacity to represent a surrogate father, while the narrator, disgusted by the petty actualities of stale middle-class life and the bleak atmosphere among the letter-writing types, senses in Esmé a saving balance between the "silly-billy" innocence of children and the squalor of adulthood. In the tearoom, neither character is fully aware of the implications of this "strangely emotional moment." But as time passes, each retrospectively achieves insight into the nature of their love, and the capacity to respond is manifested by the creation of meaningful forms of expression. Only later, with Esmé's letter and the loan of her father's watch, do we find that she fully recognizes the import of the meeting. For the narrator, the recitation of the story—the artistic process—fulfills his promise to write Esmé a story both "squalid and moving."

Salinger denies us a view of the psychological process which prompts Esmé to forward her father's watch. We do, however, witness X's emergence from a hell characterized by explicit failures of language to communicate love. While his inability to read, write, or think clearly is a result of the "suffering of being unable to love," human contact causes even further deterioration. His conversation with Clay and the letter from his brother structurally parallel X's earlier conversation with Esmé and the letter he later opens from Esmé. Here, however, these forms of communication perform exactly the opposite office, indicating that language, not founded on love and a sympathetic comprehension of another's condition, expresses negation and advances alienation. Because of his insensitivity, Clay cannot comprehend the extent and cause of X's emotional deterioration. Clay does not even understand why X sarcastically interprets Clay's reasons for killing "that pussycat in as manly a way as anybody could've under the circumstances." The conversation culminates in X's nausea, which follows Clay's most ironic failure to perceive the meaning of X's words:

"That cat was a spy. You had to take a pot shot at it. It was a very clever German midget dressed up in a cheap fur coat. So there was absolutely nothing brutal, or cruel, or dirty, or even—"

"God damn it!" Clay said, his lips thinned. "Can't you ever be *sincere?*"

X suddenly felt sick, and he swung around in his chair and grabbed the wastebasket—just in time (p. 110).

This is undoubtedly the same wastebasket which holds the torn remnants of his brother's request for souvenirs, the accouterments of the very war which threatens to destroy X's being. His brother's letter was probably sent in the unquestioned belief that the Sergeant receiving the letter would be the same one who left home. This Sergeant, however, has gone through a revolution of consciousness, profoundly altering his relation to home, self, and society. Americans back home like X's wife, mother-in-law, and brother inhabit a spatial, experiential, and psychological world which is entirely foreign to X's life. They have no way to comprehend the waste and horror which X has seen. Thus, his brother's letter accentuates distance, fails to provide relief, and moves X closer to an absolute loss of reason.

Neither callous letter, nor talking to Clay about Loretta, nor listening to Bob Hope on the radio can help X to recover his faculties. Instead, he needs personal contact with someone who has a sensitive understanding of the way war can destroy one's being. Like X, Esmé has been ravaged by the war and, emotionally, her experiences and problems are similar to the Sergeant's: she has been stripped of her former source of coherence, order, and love through the death of her parents; Sergeant X's former way of ordering experience no longer pertains to his life; both need to reconstruct their lives after being "wounded" by the war. By chance, X opens Esmé's letter and receives help from the only available source. The act of reading the letter stuns him, touching off an awareness of the significance of their meeting in the tearoom. The letter and the loan of her father's watch spring from Esmé's deep desire to express love. It is not so much the letter's stilted words or the statistics which affect X; instead, it is his deeply-felt, overwhelming experience of Esmé's love which begins his cure by inducing sleep.

"For Esmé" reflects the power of language to communicate love. Here, Salinger successfully mediates between silence and sentimentality by presenting two instances of expression—Esmé's letter to the narrator and the narrator's story "for Esmé"—which evolve from each character's comprehension of the meaning of love.[3] These forms of expression represent moral and aesthetic resolutions to the problems of human communication permeating the narrative. Unlike the endings of many classic American tales, the conclusion of "For Esmé—with Love and Squalor" fulfills the process of self-recovery rather than simply bringing the hero to a point at which he either has nowhere to go or is *about* to make use of what he has learned. "For Esmé" has closure at the same time that it suggests how the narrator will live within society, even though his experiences have taught him the inherent failure of conventional society. On the one hand, the ending of the story completes the process of therapy which began with the discovery of Esmé's letter, fulfills the promise to write her a story, and completes the office of symbolic father. As Ihab Hassan notes, the story can be looked at as a "modern epithalamium."[4] It is also a wedding gift, a parting gesture of love from father to daughter. On the other hand, the narrator has managed to gain a balanced perspective; he has found a way to avoid paralyzing isolation and survive with good humor even though living within a world dominated by the likes of his wife and mother-in-law. Even though he may be impeded from acting as he would like, he still has his art.

Communication is difficult within such a world, but possible. Salinger dramatizes this difficulty by crowding his world with people who are not so much malicious as unconscious. The best one can say about Clay, for example, is that he tries to help X. But like most characters in Salinger's fiction, Clay is impeded by his utter incapacity to transcend the values which he holds sacred and never questions. Thus, one response to the horror which threatens civilization resides in accommodating oneself completely to the stereotypical conventionalities of middle-class existence—the world of Saks, cashmere, convenient marriages, college psychology courses, war souvenirs, and complacent acceptance of army bureaucracy. But in presenting two successful expressions of love, Salinger offers an optimistic answer to the implied question: How can one respond to the void after confronting, in Esmé's words, "a method of existence that is ridiculous to say the least" (p. 113)?

Nevertheless, "For Esmé" presents the early signs in Salinger of his apparent acceptance of silence, not as a negative or cowardly retreat from the literary field, as some of his detractors would have it, but as a positive, implicit recognition of emotions that are in themselves meaningful and therefore need no expression. This story is so interesting because it confronts the difficulty of significant human communication at a time when he still seemed to believe in writing (or at least publishing). "For Esmé—with Love and Squalor" is indeed a high point in Salinger's art for many of the reasons his other commentators have noted. Most notably, though, it addresses one of the central problems of Salinger's fiction in particular and modern literature in general—the problem of finding valid forms of communication—at the same time that the story suggests that love is the force which animates expression. In a story in which love ultimately triumphs, the relationship between the narrator and Esmé embodies a beautiful, if tenuous, example of how individuals might pass through squalor to love, achieving meaningful, redemptive expression, even though the successful uses of language are a constant reminder of its general failure.

Notes

1. One can get a general sense of the work which has been done on "For Esmé" by examining the following commentaries: Frederick L. Gwynn and Joseph L. Blotner, *The Fiction of J. D. Salinger* (Pittsburgh: University of Pittsburgh Press, 1958); Henry Antole Grunwald, ed., *Salinger: A Critical and Personal Portrait* (New York: Harper and Row, 1962); James E. Bryan, in "A Reading of Salinger's For Esmé—with Love and Squalor," *Criticism*, 9 (1967), 275–288, sums up the general terms of the critical debate: "From everything that I have seen, critics have read 'For Esmé' more or less exclusively as the story of a man's miraculous salvation from war and squalor by the love of a child; and their appraisals have seemed to depend largely on their emotional response, or lack of it, to the love and squalor."

2. "For Esmé—with Love and Squalor," in *Nine Stories* (Boston: Little Brown, 1953; rpt. New York: Bantam, 1977), p. 87. Since there is no standard edition of Salinger's works, all citations will be from the Bantam paperback.

3. Ihab Hassan discusses the polarities of silence and sentimentality. See "The Rare Quixotic Gesture," in Grunwald, pp. 138–163.

4. See Hassan, p. 145. Also see Warren French's important study, *J. D. Salinger*, which has been recently revised and reissued (Boston: Twayne, 1976). French speaks directly to the quality of celebration that emanates from the story. He writes that the story dramatizes the "dynamic essence of comedy, whose secret cause might be said to be the triumphant joy occasioned by a successful communication between human beings" (p. 98).

DENNIS L. O'CONNOR

J. D. Salinger's Religious Pluralism: The Example of Raise High the Roof Beam, Carpenters

As a writer with serious religious concerns, J. D. Salinger belongs to a venerable American tradition dating from the time of Emerson and the Transcendentalists. In the company of such artists as Thoreau, Whitman, Eliot, Ginsberg, Gary Snyder, and Thomas Merton, Salinger has responded deeply to a variety of Eastern spiritualities. Although his writings appeal to a variety of audiences on several levels, most American critics of his work have fastened on psychological or sociological questions. Even so, a few voices have responded to the religious dimensions of his art. Some problems arose, however, when certain sympathetic critics analyzed his fiction in light of these religious interests. These problems were twofold: (1) his flawless Manhattanese seemed perfectly obvious and in no need of further study; and (2) the Glass family tales betrayed an "increasing" absorption in unfamiliar Oriental ideas. Whereas few critics troubled to probe Salinger's colloquial diction (thereby ignoring the subtle shifts in meaning reminiscent of Chekhov), even fewer sought to elucidate his Orientalism (usually reduced to Zen) in relation to his narrative art.

To solve this critical impasse, I propose to examine certain religious dimensions of Salinger's fiction by focusing on *Raise High the Roof Beam, Carpenters*, the first of his Glass family chronicles. Although published twenty-five years ago in *The New Yorker*, its meaning remains largely unexplored. My

From *The Southern Review* 20, no. 2 (April 1984): 316–32. Copyright © 1984 by Louisiana State University.

argument has three parts. First, I will explicate the Taoist text of Lieh-tzu which introduces the story and relate it to the subsequent narrative. Second, I will analyze the three characters (Kao, Seymour, and the nameless old man) who constitute a Taoist fellowship and reveal the riches of Salinger's religious art. Third, I will demonstrate Salinger's religious pluralism in terms of his complementary use of Taoist, Buddhist, and Christian thought.

Salinger himself suggests the direction of this study when he has Buddy Glass explain his religious pluralism. "Would it be out of order," Buddy asks, "for me to say that both Seymour's and my roots in Eastern philosophy—if I may hesitatingly call them 'roots'—were, are, planted in the New and Old Testament, Advaita Vedanta, and classical Taoism?" Indeed, I will argue, it is *not* out of order, it is the order, the very soul of his writing. "Seymour once said that all we do our whole lives is go from one piece of Holy Ground to the next. Is he *never* wrong?" The climactic affirmation of Seymour, which Buddy recalls at the end of his long struggle, is, I believe, the quintessence of Salinger's religious vision and the warrant for this study. His vision entails a reverence for language, a delight in everyday speech which ceaselessly reveals the very depths of our lives. And so I will examine Salinger's language in relation to the "piece of Holy Ground" disclosed in *Raise High*.

I

This Glass family chronicle begins curiously. Buddy Glass, Salinger's first person narrator, sets the stage by recounting in 1955 an event from 1934, when his sister Franny, ten months old, spent the night with him and Seymour during a "siege" of the mumps. Awakened by Franny's crying, Buddy finds Seymour soothing his sister by reading aloud a Taoist tale. When Buddy objects that she's only an infant, Seymour replies, "They have ears. They can hear." By alluding to a biblical injunction about childlike reception of the word of God, Seymour stresses the seriousness of his action, the sacredness of the Taoist text, and the religious pluralism that characterizes Salinger's fiction.

In complementary distinction to the biblical emphasis upon hearing and responding to God's word, this Taoist tale stresses spiritual insight and the difference between routine adult misperception and childlike vision. The selection offered without citation is from Lionel Giles's translation, *Taoist Teachings from the Book of Lieh-tzu*, and forms part of the eighth and final chapter, "Explaining Conjunctions." Salinger quotes this tale verbatim because, with Seymour's diary, it illumines his entire narrative. I will now try to explicate the relation between these two works by exploring the Taoist background and Salinger's unique appropriation of it in his story.

In Lieh-tzu's parable, when Duke Mu asked Po-Lo, his aged judge of horses, to recommend a worthy successor, he replied: "A good horse can be picked out by its general build and appearance. But the superlative horse— one that raises no dust and leaves no tracks—is something evanescent and fleeting, elusive as thin air ... my sons can tell a good horse when they see one, but they cannot tell a superlative horse." He then recommended Chiu-fang Kao, "a hawker of fuel and vegetables." Dispatched to a remote region for such a steed, Kao reported after three months that he had found one. And, upon demand, he described it as a dun-colored mare. But when a coal black stallion arrived, Duke Mu complained to Po-Lo that Kao could not even distinguish color and sex. Delighted, Po-Lo exclaimed, "Ah, then he is worth ten thousand of me. ... Kao keeps in mind the spiritual mechanism. In making sure of the essential, he forgets the homely details; intent on the inward qualities, he loses sight of the external ... he has it within him to judge something better than horses." Drawing a parallel between Kao and Seymour, Buddy laments his brother's absence (through suicide): "Since the bridegroom's retirement from the scene, I haven't been able to think of anybody whom I'd care to send out to look for horses in his stead."

Lieh-tzu's parable, like the earlier works of Lao Tzu and Chuang Tzu, envisions a man living in the *Tao*, the Heavenly Way of perfect freedom and harmony with nature, where one loses self-consciousness and becomes as soft as water, as yielding as a woman, as free as a child, as unformed as a block of wood. Entering this emptiness without limit, form, or name, one loses any previous identity as a separate self. Now emptied of this false self (the acquisitive empirical ego with all its desires and illusions—the "old man" in St. Paul's sense), the person opens up to the Way which embraces all of being and non-being. Thus, a man "lost in *Tao*" has the spiritual freedom to envision the superlative horse, for only a visionary would ignore color and sex (shorthand for all human criteria) to judge things in the light of *Tao*. Kao sees deeply, while Duke Mu and everyone, lost in the obvious, miss what matters. The horse actually symbolizes one's deepest self dwelling in *Tao*, for the steed's elusiveness suggests the Way's characteristic transcendence of all language and objectification. According to the *Tao Te Ching* of Lao Tzu, "There are ways but the Way is uncharted ... nameless indeed in the source of creation. ... The secret waits for the insight of eyes unclouded by longing; those ... bound by desire see only the outward container." Graced with such insight, Kao glimpses his innermost heart, the evanescent superlative horse of the human spirit. His vision, born of inward stillness that "raises no dust and leaves no tracks," recalls Lao Tzu's poetic description of the *Tao*'s simplicity and lightness: "A good runner leaves no tracks. ... A good knot is tied without rope and cannot be loosed."

II

Buddy's deceptively casual statement about Seymour's "retirement" leaving him unable "to think of anybody whom I'd care to send out to look for horses in his stead" introduces the pivotal Taoist fellowship of Kao, Seymour, and the nameless old man who befriends the narrator on his brother's wedding day. These three visionaries suggest the religious depth which interprets and tempers Buddy's narrative, whose central themes include true versus false vision; and oppressive societal demands for "normalcy" versus the uncategorical way of the artist-seer living in the *Tao*.

Having considered Kao in light of Lieh-tzu's parable, we turn now to Seymour Glass, the true subject of Buddy's narrative and the corrective lens through which we understand the brothers. Avoiding common classifications and misjudgments, Seymour, like Kao, lives in the Heavenly Way. Chuang-Tzu's description of the Man of *Tao* suggests Seymour's own personality:

> The non-action of the wise man is not inaction. . . .
> The sage is quiet because he is not moved. . . .
> Still water is like glass.
> The heart of the wise man is tranquil.
> It is the mirror of heaven and earth
> The glass of everything.
> Emptiness, stillness, tranquility, tastelessness,
> Silence, non-action: this is the level of heaven and earth
> This is the perfect Tao. Wise men find here
> Their resting place.
> Resting they are empty.

By resting in the *Tao*, Seymour radiates the truth of his name: seeing more, he acts in a non-intervening way until his presence is as clear as glass. In Taoist terms, this action is *wu-wei*, literally "non-doing," that is, he acts naturally, inconspicuously, and spontaneously. Thus, his actions seem formless and empty, as aimless and "unproductive" as passing clouds or rain. In fact, the Chinese use water, the epitome of *wu-wei*'s dynamic, to symbolize the gracious humility of *Tao*:

> The highest goodness, water-like,
> Does good to everything and goes
> Unmurmuring to places men despise;
> But so, is close in nature to the Way.

This imagery recalls the biblical image of rain falling on the just and unjust as a sign of God's all-inclusive mercy.

Seymour's "water-like," non-judgmental *wu-wei* informs his relationship to his bride and her family. A diary entry, written before the wedding, exemplifies his understanding acceptance of Muriel Fedder and her parents:

> The familiarity between Muriel and her mother struck me as being so beautiful when we were all sitting in the living room. They know each other's weaknessess ... and pick at them with their eyes. ... When they argue, there can be no danger of a permanent rift, because they're Mother and Daughter. A terrible and beautiful phenomenon to watch. Yet there are times ... I wish Mr. Fedder were more conversationally active. Sometimes I feel I need him. Sometimes, in fact, when I come in the front door, it's like entering a kind of untidy, secular, two-woman convent. Sometimes when I leave, I have a peculiar feeling that both M and her mother have stuffed my pockets with little bottles and tubes containing lipstick, rouge, hair nets, deodorants, and so on. I feel overwhelmingly grateful to them, but I don't know what to do with their invisible gifts.

Where Buddy reviles his enemies and then withdraws into self-pity, Seymour accepts without winking or accusation. He senses that Mr. Fedder is castrated, that masculinity has no chance in this "two-woman convent," and that mother and daughter are set on domesticating him as well. Indeed, his imagining their stuffing him with "feminine notions," the clichés and accoutrements of their derivative identities, indicates his awareness of their effort to appropriate his manhood. This "terrible and beautiful phenomenon" would make him "normal," that is, one of them, by pressuring him into psychoanalysis, a treatment that promises psychic mutilation for the poet. Nevertheless, despite their efforts to "overhaul" him, he remains happy and open.

Seymour's mysterious equanimity, which neither Buddy, nor Muriel, nor Mrs. Fedder, nor apparently the majority of Salinger's critics can understand, makes sense from a Taoist perspective. In fact, Salinger offers a Taoist clue in the first diary entry, where Seymour contrasts his tranquility with the distress of his fellow soldiers fainting from the cold. "I have no circulation, no pulse. Immobility is my home. The tempo of 'the Star-Spangled Banner' and I are in perfect understanding. To me, its rhythm is a romantic waltz." This serenity recalls Lieh-tzu's meditation on the sage: "holding fast to his purest energies ... he will unify his nature ... until he penetrates to the place where things are created. If you can be like this, the Heaven inside you will keep its integrity, the spirit inside you will have no flaws ... the sage hides himself in Heaven, therefore no thing can harm him." Living in the Way, Seymour need not choose between military and romantic music. As Lieh-tzu says, "the

man ... in harmony is absolutely the same as other things, and no thing suc-
ceeds in wounding or obstructing him." Precisely because Seymour dwells
in the *Tao*, he is unrushed, unfatigued, tranquil in the emptiness of *wu-wei*
which entails "freedom from the accretions of desire and the influence of the
senses." Thus, his peace presupposes a flexible detachment that overcomes all
obstacles. Huai Nan Tzu aptly described those resting in *wu-wei* as possess-
ing "a yielding mind; nevertheless their work is invincible."

If Taoist thought clarifies Seymour's serenity, it also explains his apparent "formlessness." Buddy's reference to him in *Seymour*, as a "Formless Bastard," provides another Taoist clue. As Chuang-Tzu observes, "[the True
Master] can act—that is certain. Yet I cannot see his form. He has identity
but no form." If Seymour eludes "normal," rational categories, neither defense
nor attack makes any difference. Thus Chuang-Tzu comments that "to men
such as these [who dwell in the Way], how could there be any question of
putting life first or death last? ... Idly they roam beyond the dust and dirt:
they wander free and easy in the service of inaction [*wu-wei*]. Why should
they fret about the ceremonies of the vulgar world ... ?" This freedom from
competition and self-aggrandizement (the "dust and dirt" of appetitive striving) transforms Seymour's mind into a polished mirror whose emptiness
effortlessly reflects what it sees and is. Such inner clarity manifests itself in
contemplative detachment, what the eleventh century Taoist painter, Mi Yu-
jen, called "the wisdom of the eye." "When we reach maturity in painting,"
he wrote, "we are not attached to the mundane world. ... Whenever in the
quiet of my room with my legs crossed I sit silently then I feel that I float up
and down with the blue sky, vast and silent." Such intuition of "the interfu-
sion of the self with the universe" and the harmony of form and formlessness (the sky, like an uncarved block or running water, is a Taoist symbol of
formlessness), being and non-being (*wu*), characterizes *wu-wei*. In his recent
study, *Creativity and Taoism*, Chang Chung-yuan argues that *wu-wei* "does
not mean quiescence after action has ceased, but quiescence forever in action."
Thus, Seymour's own water-like formlessness is dynamic, but, like his full
name, it serves as a mirror and a lens to quietly reflect and focus the flowing
world. Chuang-Tzu's meditation on formlessness unfolds this inner richness.
According to this greatest of Chinese philosophers, "man alone is more than
an object. Though, like objects, he has form and semblance, he is not limited
to form. He is more. He can attain to formlessness. When he is beyond form
and semblance, beyond 'this' and 'that'. ... where is the conflict? He will rest in
his eternal place which is no-place. He will be hidden in his own unfathom-
able secret. His vitality, his power hide in secret Tao."

Before discussing the third member of the Taoist fellowship, the childlike nameless one who befriends Buddy, I should briefly mention two other

Glass family members who embody this Taoist ideal of yielding formlessness. As little children Franny and Zooey manifest the freedom of the Heavenly Way while appearing on the radio program called "It's a Wise Child." The first incident, which Boo Boo mentions in her letter to Buddy, involves Franny's recollecting how "she used to fly all around the apartment when she was four and no one was home." Since Buddy prefaced his narrative with Franny's claim that she remembers hearing Lieh-tzu's parable, it seems fitting that she should imitate the man who claimed "my mind concentrated and my body relaxed . . . I drifted with the wind East or West, like a leaf . . . and never knew whether it was the wind that rode me or I that rode the wind." Chuang-Tzu uses this essential emptiness, formlessness, and sameness of the *Tao* to characterize a child. The second incident concerns Zooey's response to the questions of sameness. "He said it would be very nice to come home and be in the wrong house. To eat dinner with the wrong people by mistake, sleep in the wrong bed by mistake, and kiss everybody goodbye in the morning thinking they were your own family. He said he even wished everybody in the world looked exactly alike. He said you'd keep thinking everybody you met was your wife or your mother or father, and people would always be throwing their arms around each other wherever they went." Aside from its Taoist qualities of harmony, pre-reflective unity, and *wu-wei*, Zooey's vision also contains eschatological, Messianic, and eucharistic implications. In the biblical vision of the heavenly Jerusalem, when Christ will be all in all at the end of time, we shall see God face to face and know him even as we ourselves are known. Released from the bonds of sin and death, we will live in our glorified risen bodies as Jesus's brothers and sisters, the flesh and blood of his mystical body at last whole and harmonious. Within this eucharistic fellowship of unending love, we will be God's true image and likeness, at once profoundly ourselves and perfectly intimate with every other being in his creation.

Placing Zooey's religious vision in the context of Seymour's evening with the Fedders, Salinger emphasizes its relation to the Vedantic passage which concludes Seymour's diary. "I've been reading a miscellany of Vedanta all day. Marriage partners are to serve each other. Elevate, help, teach, strengthen each other, but above all *serve*. Raise their children honorably, lovingly, and with detachment. A child is a guest in the house, to be loved and respected— never possessed, since he belongs to God." Harmonizing with both the gospel teaching about welcoming children in the name of Jesus and his heavenly Father and the resulting Christian monastic custom of receiving each guest as another Christ, this Vedantic injunction stresses compassionate service that coincides with Taoist reverence for creation and childlike spontaneity.

Like Kao and Seymour, the third member of the Taoist fellowship manifests a serene freedom which matches Chuang-Tzu's description of the "Man of Spirit, the Nameless One." He can only be identified as Muriel's father's uncle, a tiny deaf-mute, whose silent composure underscores the tumultuous distress of those around him. When we first meet him in the limousine filled with wedding guests, he is sitting next to Bunny. Unlike the Matron of Honor, however, he has plenty of room ("his silk hat cleared the roof of the car by a good four or five inches") and creates psychic space for Buddy through unaccusing silence. Diminutive, he seems unique among the suffering "grownups," especially since his stature corresponds to an egolessness that spares him anguish. Buddy, on the other hand, suffering from pleurisy and pressed into service as a doorman after the abortive ceremony ("like . . . a young giant with a cough"), bangs his head against the car roof. Miserable, he still rejoices in the nameless man's presence. "When I'd originally loaded the car, I'd a passing impulse to pick him up bodily and insert him gently through the window." Concentrated and present as none of his self-conscious companions can be, the old man resembles the Taoist ideal of the Perfect Man who "has no self." Chuang-Tzu distinguishes such serenity by affirming that "great understanding is broad and unhurried; little understanding is cramped and busy. Great words are clear and limpid; little words are shrill and quarrelsome." The Nameless One embodies this opposition to unavailing distress: "Let your mind wander in simplicity, blend your spirit with the vastness, follow along with things the way they are, and make no room for personal views." And his attention certainly suggests a Taoist childlike attitude as well as Franny's own analogous receptiveness to Seymour's reading. Thus, he calmly just sits "staring very severely straight ahead of him," reminiscent of Chuang-Tzu's characterization of a "childlike stare" embracing mystery as "the understanding of that which is not to be understood," namely the ineffable *Tao* itself. As the Nameless One, he is egolessness and silence incarnate. Mute and detached, he suggests both Kao's forgetfulness of the inessential as well as Seymour's visionary presence, a dwelling in immediate formless simplicity that transcends the dichotomy of subject and object. According to Lu Chi-p'u, "freedom from words, or *hai-yen*, means that *Tao* expresses itself; this is called the essence of nature. When one listens to it, nothing is heard. It is the state of namelessness and selflessness."

Salinger underscores the nameless one's detachment when he contrasts his composure with the huge Matron of Honor's childish "little plaint of frustration and pique." "The delay didn't seem to affect him. His standard of comportment for sitting in the rear seat of cars . . . seemed to be fixed. . . . You just sat very erect . . . and you stared ferociously ahead at the windshield. . . . If Death . . . stepped miraculously through the glass and came in after you, in all probability you just got up and went along with him." Such detachment echoes Chuang-Tzu's prescription for living in the *Tao*: "being upright, you will be still; being still, you will be enlightened; being enlightened, you will be empty; and being empty, you will do nothing, and yet there will be nothing that is not done." The nameless one's inaction conforms to Chuang-Tzu's teaching: "the inaction of heaven is its purity, the inaction of earth is its peace." Calmly facing death, he resembles the Taoist ideal of the child who "stares all day without blinking its eyes—it has no preferences in the world of externals."

Nameless, useless, simply himself, he transcends classification, yet he alone among the wedding guests communicates without acrimony or pretense. A single written word of acceptance, "Delighted," expresses his whole being in an act of *disponibilité* that affirms the underlying Taoist perspective. Chuang-Tzu urges liberation from worldly concerns because conventional values impede this mystical freedom and keep one shackled. Hence, if one wishes freedom, one must practice *wu-wei* which creates harmony by letting all human actions "become as spontaneous as those of the natural world." And Taoism values such childlike immediacy and nonconflictual action because the self, once empty of egocentric striving, has no need to compete. Like Kao or the superlative horse, the nameless one interacts harmoniously with the universe and leaves no trace: being emptiness itself, he creates space for all.

According to Chuang-Tzu, this emptiness necessitates "fasting of the heart," whose goal is inner unity.

> "This means ... hearing with the spirit, with your whole being ... [which] is not limited to any one faculty, to the ear, or to the mind. Hence it demands the emptiness of all the faculties. ... Then the whole being listens. There is then a direct grasp of what is right there before you that can never be heard with the ear or understood with the mind. Fasting of the heart ... frees you from limitation and from preoccupation ... and begets unity and freedom.
>
> Look at this window: ... because of it the whole room is full of light. So when the faculties are empty, the heart ... full of light ... becomes an influence by which others are secretly transformed.

Thus centered and empty in the Taoist sense, the nameless old man, like Kao, is appropriately cut off from the inessential. Salinger symbolically indicates this "fasting of the heart" by depriving him of speech, hearing, and preferences. Death and life, movement and immobility, solitude and companionship, are alike to him because he, like Lieh-tzu, rests in the emptiness of *wu-wei*. And this immersion in the *Tao*'s simplicity makes him a window and a refuge that secretly transforms Buddy.

Salinger emphasizes the old man's divine quality through Buddy's drunken questions. "Don't you have a home to go to? Who looks after you? The pigeons in the Park?" Such radical homelessness, unconditional dependence upon God's care, and joyful lack of self-concern ("in response to these provocative questions, my host toasted me with renewed gusto") recall the gospel passages about the blessed freedom of the Beatitudes, the lilies of the fields, and the Son of Man having no place to rest his head. Yet here again Salinger's religious pluralism makes us aware of further ranges of meaning within this image of homelessness. Indeed, this wandering pilgrim suggests not only the Taoist Nameless One and the biblical and liturgical theme of the people of God journeying toward the heavenly Jerusalem: he also alludes to the ancient Indian ideal of *sannyāsa*, homeless existence as a wandering mendicant, the final stage of traditional Hindu ascesis. As a type of *sannyāsi*, he practices self-denial characteristic of one who has abandoned all human security and certitude and now searches for the infinite. Ministering to Buddy's need, he manifests the Hindu values of *ahimsā* (nonviolence) and *brahma-carya* (quest for God), as well as the Buddhist perfection of *karunā* (compassion), *maitri* (loving kindness), *prājña* (wisdom), and *śūnyatā* (emptiness). Moreover, his self-surrender suggests Christ's own *kenosis*, the total self-emptying to save humankind.

The old man's spiritual nature suggests his essential relation to Seymour. This spiritual kinship appears when Buddy, anxious lest he be recognized as Seymour's brother, glances at his friend and notices "almost with gratitude ... that his feet didn't quite touch the floor. They looked like old and valued friends of mine." Salinger further strengthens this connection when Buddy lyingly tells Bunny that Seymour "was a chiropodist," denoting a person who treats both hands and feet, organs of special significance for Seymour. One immediately thinks of Sybil and Seymour's feet in "A Perfect Day for Bananafish"; Charlotte Mayhew's expressing pleasure over Seymour's performance during the radio show by tramping on his feet ("He loved people who stepped on his feet"); and the discussion in *Seymour* of Seymour's hands in relation to his being a Jew. Throughout these fictions, hands and feet function as synecdoches indicating a person's psychic state. This synecdoche figures in Seymour's diary when Mrs. Fedder wants him to undergo analysis after he marries Muriel. "If or when, I do start going to an analyst, I hope to God he has the foresight to let a dermatologist sit in on consultation. *A hand specialist.* I have scars on my hands from touching certain people." These scars witness his extraordinary openness, his refusal to exclude anyone from his life, even as the nameless one's concentrated silence and childlike availability reveal a whole-hearted participation in the *Tao*.

The old man's kinship with Seymour becomes comically clear when Buddy hysterically denounces Bunny for attacking his brother. Reporting Mrs. Fedder's slur "that this Seymour ... was a latent homosexual" and "a really schizoid personality," she then accuses him of "having never *grown up*" and of acting like "an absolute raving maniac of some crazy kind." Buddy's reaction is understandably, but absurdly, intemperate: "I said I didn't give a good God damn what Mrs. Fedder ... or any professional dilettante or amateur bitch had to say.... I said that not one God-damn person ... had ever seen him for what he really was. A poet, for God's sake. And I mean a *poet*. If he never wrote a line of poetry, he could still flash what he had at you with the back of his ear if he wanted to." The only thing that stopped Buddy's self-indulgent attack was the sound of the toilet being flushed by the nameless old man. Now given this bizarre wedding reception, we probably should not be surprised to find a shouting match between the matron of honor and the surrogate groom that ends with a toilet being flushed by a nameless deaf-mute. His nonverbal contribution to a parodic epithalamion seems ironically appropriate, especially since Buddy describes his speech as "the polluted stream of invective I'd loosed on them." Besides the scatological humor reminiscent of Chaucer and the chapel scene in *The Catcher in the Rye*, the nameless one's spontaneous offering has a deeper significance. Buddy's harangue about Seymour's not being recognized as a poet recalls his earlier response to the old man's "Delighted," when, as he says, "I ... tried to show by my expression that all of us in the car knew a poem when we saw one." "The universally familiar sound of plumbing," the old man's comic "poem," identifies him with Seymour, whose transcendent poetry did not rely on words either.

In harmony with the Taoist teaching that the Heavenly Way is just as much present in excrement as it is in the most sublime human experiences, the old man's poem prompts Buddy to let go his anger and judgmentalism. As such, it recalls Chuang-Tzu's invitation to accompany him to "the palace of Nowhere where all the many things are One." The "palace of Nowhere" in "the land of Non-Doing" suggests Zooey's intuition of *wu-wei*, where indeed "all the many things are One." This confluence of all living things in turn evokes Eliot's "still-point of the turning world" and the eschatological vision of the messianic banquet, where all creation shall find nourishment and rest.

III

Rather than blurring or collapsing different Oriental and Western traditions, Salinger's religious pluralism finds artistic expression in a respectful and playful interaction of distinct layers of meaning. This playful respect, which distinguishes his aesthetic and relates it to Taoist and Buddhist practice, appears in his customary use of simple words and images to convey complex themes. The ending of *Raise High* is a case in point. Waking to find the old man gone, Buddy concludes that only "his empty glass, and cigar end in the pewter ashtray, indicated that he had ever existed. I still rather think his cigar end should have been forwarded on to Seymour, the usual run of wedding gifts being what it is. Just the cigar in a small, nice box. Possibly with a blank sheet of paper enclosed, by way of explanation." In this final part of my argument, I will demonstrate how these three objects—the glass, cigar, and sheet of paper "by way of explanation"—reveal Salinger's aesthetic and the story's pattern of densely-woven religious meaning. But before attempting these interconnections, we must examine the objects individually.

The empty glass has an extraordinary polysemous richness. Symbolizing egolessness and self-transcendence, it establishes the final link between the Nameless One and Seymour Glass. Like the ecstatic Seymour, the old man (also a poet) has gone beyond ordinary human modes of hearing, understanding, and presence. So like Lao Tzu disappearing into the West, Lieh-tzu riding the wind, Kao immersing himself in the vision of spiritual things, and Mi Yu-jen floating "up and down with the sky," he abandons everything in simple detachment. Thus, in harmony with Chuang-Tzu's "fasting of the heart," his empty glass functions as a clear window clarifying Salinger's meaning through a metaphor of the mind and heart disciplined, still, and "full of light." This metaphor further suggests the "emptiness" or perfect freedom of the human faculties now resting in *Tao*.

Besides indicating the spiritual qualities common to these two poets, the glass also stands as a synecdoche of their paradoxical space-time presence in the story. The bridegroom, for example, never appears but his absence dominates the entire day. Indeed, his fatal "retirement" from the scene apparently colors Buddy's art and oppresses his very being. This powerful absence moves us forward and backward through time as Salinger's allusively structured narrative shuttles us between 1934 (Franny hears Seymour read Lieh-tzu), 1942 (the wedding day), 1948 (Seymour's suicide), and 1955 (Buddy's puzzling through these events). But if Seymour's absence proves curiously palpable, the old man's presence is about as elusive as the superlative horse. Remote from the common distress, he is egolessly cool in their inferno. Since both poets are paradoxically present and absent, the empty glass—like the absent Glass—suggests a common passing beyond into the "palace of Nowhere."

The empty glass indicating their common passing recalls Chuang-Tzu's symbol of the empty boat and the freedom of living "with Tao in the land of the great Void." His description reveals the significance of these two present-absent "empty glass" poets. "If you can empty your boat," writes Chuang-Tzu, "crossing the river of the world, no one will oppose you. . . . Whoever can free himself from achievement . . . will flow like Tao, unseen . . . like life itself with no name and no home . . . leaving no trace." The empty glass, then, in its Taoist aspects suggests an egoless transcendence of human cares and illusions.

From a Buddhist viewpoint, the empty glass offers additional riches. Whereas Chuang-Tzu portrays "the heart of the wise man" as "the mirror of heaven and earth, the glass of everything," Buddhists interpret a clear mirror as a symbol of *Nirvāna*, the intuition of absolute undifferentiation of pure suchness (Skt. *tathātā*). The Chinese Zen Buddhist Master, Shen-hui, understands suchness as "our original Mind of which we are conscious; yet there is neither the one who is conscious nor that of which there is consciousness." Thus the mirror (or the empty glass/absent Glass in *Raise High*) signifies a mind returned to its primal clarity, released from all dualisms and ego-consciousness. Hence, the Chinese Buddhist dictum, "the mind of a child is the mind of a Buddha," never focuses on romantic illusions of childhood innocence but directs us toward that seeing which makes us a Buddha. By abandoning adult misperception to attain enlightenment (*bodhi*), one becomes in a sense a mirror of suchness or "formlessness." As an empty glass or mirror, we recover our Buddha-nature, that is, we awaken to the undifferentiated totality that our only true Self is.

The Buddhist viewpoint also explains Buddy's partial enlightenment and discloses a wider circle of corresponding spiritual traditions. Enlightenment occurs in the intuition of the essential "emptiness" (Skt. *śūnyatā*) or interdependent contingency of everything. When this vision of *śūnyatā* discloses one's Buddha-nature, one grasps the essential emptiness of the human ego striving to be dominant. Accordingly, when Buddy wakes from his stupor to find the old man gone, I think Salinger implies some degree of enlightenment because the glass, cigar, and blank paper are positive and negative symbols of emptiness, *Nirvāna*, and suchness. On the one hand, they embody the exhaustion of ordinary communication, pointing us toward the extinction of subject-object modes of perception and relation, while, on the other hand, they positively suggest the consequent recovery of our Buddha-nature. This primal unity resembles the Taoist state symbolized by a virgin block of wood (*p'u*) connoting "simplicity and genuineness in spirit and heart." Mencius himself alludes to this Taoist value when he claims "the great man is one who does not lose his child's heart." This "child's heart" also accords with the Christian perfection of "purity of heart," which St. Isaac of Syria, in a passage from *The Philokalia*, another favorite text of Salinger, glosses as "compassion for all beings." Finally, this circle of correspondences becomes complete when we realize that the essence of Buddha-nature is the perfect union of compassion (*karunā*) and wisdom (*prājñā*).

The poetic and religious richness of this circle of correspondences relates the empty glass to the cigar end and the blank sheet of paper. In this context, the cigar end recalls the root meaning of *Nirvāna*, a putting out, an extinction of all craving (*tanha*) and ignorance (*avidyā*). Like the Buddha who attained *Nirvāna* after extinguishing the passions, the old man passes beyond all worldly fetters and in so doing recalls *Tathāgata* (literally, "he who is thus gone"), an honorific title of the Buddha. In this passage, he leaves behind an *extinguished* cigar end, emblematic of the human condition now transcended. This cigar *end* intimates the completeness and finality of his victory. As a symbol of the old man's utter calm in the face of Death, the *cigar* also discloses some further meanings of *Nirvāna*, namely, "liberated from existence; calmed, quieted, vanishing from sight [one thinks of the "evanescent" superlative horse and Seymour himself]; eternal bliss [cf. the Nameless One's "Delighted"]; complete satisfaction or pleasure; and deliverance" (Monier-Williams' *Sanskrit–English Dictionary*).

The uselessness of this extinguished cigar is analogous to the wordless emptiness of the blank sheet of paper enclosed "by way of explanation." Its "emptiness" bespeaks the Buddhist intuition of *śūnyatā*, the negative side of suchness, which words can never communicate because it transcends the subject-object, knower-known dichotomies implicit in ordinary discourse. Its nonsensical blankness also signals Buddy's comic participation in the Taoist-Zen Buddhist tradition of nonrational dialogue and transcendent silence. Reaching the limits of narration and narrativity, Buddy trusts we will accompany him in a polysemous communion of implied meanings. Here, "intent on the inward qualities," we "lose sight of the external" and become Salinger's "amateur reader" who shares (in every sense) the dedication of and to the work. And as dedicated "amateur" readers, we share the silence of implied meanings which the blank paper symbolizes and completes. Explaining nothing, it directs us beyond ordinary syntactic and semantic constraints to the Nothing of *śūnyatā* and *wu-wei*. Thus, this blankness does not eliminate meaning but rather transposes it to another key, where it becomes a metaphor of and inducement to Buddha consciousness, a vehicle for provoking enlightenment. As a vehicle of enlightenment, this blank explanation both complements and refers back to the empty glass and extinguished cigar end as well as to the Taoist block of wood (*p'u*), the old man's namelessness, the Buddhist vision of ineffable suchness, and Seymour's "retirement" and wordless poetry. All these instances of apparent blankness, absence, and semantic transposition make sense within a pluralistic religious perspective open to the mystery of revelatory silence, which is really a form of prayer, a communion with the divine.

Faced with the complex religious pluralism which structures Salinger's Glass family chronicles, we should not expect to eliminate the mystery surrounding Seymour Glass's life and death. While thinking about these issues, I came across a comment by a twentieth-century Carthusian contemplative that seemed particularly pertinent. According to this anonymous monk of La Valsainte, a monastery high in the Swiss Alps, "All life is fraught with mystery both in its origins and in its workings. Thus the spiritual life, which is the most mysterious of all, life's very essence, is the most hidden and the least explicable; for it is too simple and too infinite, preventing words and beyond expression." Now given Salinger's immersion in spiritual questions and the congruent interests and callings of his characters (Seymour's *dharma* as a *mukta*, poet, and seer; Waker's vocation as a Carthusian; Franny and Zooey's questing after God; Buddy's attempt to be his brother's keeper), I believe the creator of the Glass family might agree with this view of religious mystery. And if this explication of *Raise High* can only take us to the edge of mystery, it should stress how much this story abides and has meaning within this mystery. We have already noted, for example, the mystical realities implied through the cigar, the empty glass, and the sheet of paper. Now, in conclusion, I will suggest how this blank paper poetically entails Seymour and Muriel's marriage bed, Buddy's relation to his brother, and Boo Boo's rash judgment of the bride.

The blank paper symbolizes the "inconclusive" narrative, the unfulfilled possibilities of the wedding celebration, and the range of suspended meanings that make this text so difficult to interpret. Of all the characters and issues in this story, the bride herself remains a total blank, a *terra incognita*. And here again Salinger returns us to the beginning, where Boo Boo describes Muriel as "a zero . . . but terrific looking. I don't actually know she's a zero." As amateur readers, we've learned that we *know* only by penetrating externals. She may come across as a "zero," but to one who is "ecstatically happy" and "sees more" than routine adult misperception allows, Muriel fully deserves his love. Yet here Salinger may be hinting that sexual passion limits Seymour's vision. The poem of Sappho which Boo Boo writes in soap on Seymour's bathroom mirror serves not only as a parodic epithalamion (it anticipates messages traditionally written on the windshield of the honeymoon couple's car), it also provides the title of Salinger's story. Thus, the poem seems significant, especially since it obscures (no matter how delightfully) Seymour's mirror and therefore seems to portend some psychic confusion. Sappho describes the bridegroom as "taller far than a tall man," which recent scholarship interprets as having appropriate ithyphallic connotations. Whether or not Muriel's extraordinary beauty and his own presumably intense sexual desire blind Seymour, it is certain that her name means "bright sea," and in his eyes she is nothing less than Aphrodite. Salinger may be ironically invoking Muriel's mythical identity when he has his hero commit suicide on a twin

bed opposite his sleeping wife at a seaside resort in Florida. Accurately or
not, the suicidal visionary now refers to his wife as "Miss Spiritual Tramp."
Finally, one could argue that Muriel Fedder, as the daughter of Rhea, whose
name recalls the Great Mother Goddess and the death and castration of her
multitudinous lovers, unwittingly "fetters" Seymour, binding him to her limit-
ing, unspiritual world.

　　While this negative view of Muriel as a spiritual "zero" seems initially
plausible, I think Salinger's critique of adult misperception must balance any
such interpretation. Boo Boo's description suggests the many senses of *śūnya*,
the Sanskrit etymon for "zero," used by Buddhist metaphysicians and mystics to describe ultimate wisdom. *Śunya* or *śūnyatā*, "emptiness," paradoxically
denotes fullness, limitless presence, radical interrelatedness, and the perfectly
ordinary. According to D. T. Suzuki, *śūnyatā*, as "zero," does not mean "a
mathematical symbol. It is the infinite—a storehouse or womb (*garbha*) of all
possible good or values." Thus Seymour marries Muriel, this Aphrodite-zero,
and thereby embraces the Taoist life of indiscrimination, mirroring its essential formlessness, its egolessness that seems foolishness but is truly wisdom.
By specifying a *sheet* of paper, rather than a piece or a *page*, Salinger directs
our attention back to the marriage bed and Seymour's diary which Buddy
thrusts in anger among the discarded sheets. In this sense, the blank sheet of
paper may indicate Buddy's forgiveness of Seymour and his own kinship with
the Nameless One. Transcending judgmental language, if only for a moment,
Buddy's wordless gesture could suggest a movement toward renunciation of
his anger and the related desire to control Seymour. The religious plenum
which nourishes and structures this story leads me to suggest that the blank
sheet of paper, which, like Indra's net, perfectly reflects every other facet of
the narrative, is both comic gift and suitable memento of the wedding, the
couple, and Seymour's vision: not lack, but fullness, a polysemy beyond words,
an intuitive suchness which involves the sacred mysteries of sexuality, death,
silence, and wisdom.

ANTHONY KAUFMAN

"Along this road goes no one": Salinger's "Teddy" and the Failure of Love

1

The reputation of J. D. Salinger rests largely on two relatively short works: *The Catcher in the Rye* and *Nine Stories*. The *Nine Stories* collection is brilliant, but it is seemingly marred by the final story, "Teddy." Salinger himself seems to dismiss the story. In what can be read as his own commentary, Salinger, through his arch, uncertain disguise as Buddy Glass, in *Seymour— An Introduction*, calls "Teddy" "an ex*cept*ionally Haunting, Memorable, unpleasantly controversial, and thoroughly unsuccessful short story" (205). Critics have generally agreed, objecting particularly to the seemingly contrived character of Teddy who claims that he is a 10-year-old perfect master, equipped with clairvoyance, and to the ambiguity of the conclusion, where it is not entirely clear what happens.[1]

But despite these seemingly well-founded objections, I will argue that the story is highly successful—indeed deeply moving—when we understand that "Teddy" is the story not of a cool and detached mystical prodigy, but of an unloved, frightened 10-year-old. Teddy has reacted defensively to an exploitative adult world by intuitively developing the persona of the mystic and clairvoyant both to gain the love he desperately needs and, paradoxically, to distance himself from his uncaring family and the grown-up world. Although critics have in general taken straight the premise that Teddy is indeed a little swami and analyzed in depth the importance of Zen to this

---

From *Studies in Short Fiction* 35 (1998): 129–40. Copyright © 1998 by Newberry College.

story and to Salinger generally, it is only when we peel away the overlay of mysticism that the story becomes coherent and moving—and only then does "Teddy" become a valid and satisfactory conclusion to the *Nine Stories* collection. We will see, however, that the mystic elements of the story are indeed crucial, although not in the way that critics have suggested.

What has happened is this: in defensive reaction to the egotism, love-lessness, and incessant hostility of his parents toward each other and toward their children, and reinforced by his sense of the vulgarity, selfishness, and materialism of grown-up life, Teddy has instinctively felt his way to creating his persona of the mystic savant. That is, based on his precocious acquaintance (perhaps through Alan Watts and Dr. Suzuki?) in Eastern philosophy, he has convinced himself (and some of the grown-up world) of his mystic powers.[2] The benefits of this disguise to Teddy are several: not only can he withdraw from his parents, and the adult world more generally, and ward off feelings of anxiety and depression that any 10 year old might experience in his difficult family situation—he can also vent his feelings of anger toward them through his pose of studied responsibility and tolerant acceptance of their faults. He can feel distanced from a frightening world, sought-after, superior. He can believe that he has control of his 10-year-old world. His disguise of perfect master (although extreme) has affinities with the defensive use of the imagination by other children in the *Nine Stories* collection: Ramona's imaginary lover and defender Jimmy in "Uncle Wiggily in Connecticut," the precocious adult-like attitude of Esmé, and the pretentious self-presentation of De Daumier-Smith.

Thus the story "Teddy" works in two ways, both to portray Salinger's characteristic child victim (and thus it forms a satiric comment on the adult world), and also to create an interesting and credible study of the way in which a 10-year-old has intuitively defended himself against the ego, anger, and indifference that his parents and the adult world have inflicted upon him. In its portrayal of the underloved child, "Teddy" embodies the Salinger masterplot as seen in *Catcher* and the other stories of *Nine Stories*.

Yet Salinger makes another, highly important use of the mysticism Teddy explains and advocates. The doctrine of love he preaches represents a valid and necessary response to the world and suggests the author's putative answer to the problems seen throughout *Nine Stories* and, indeed, all of his published fiction. In reaction to the harshness of American life, it is necessary to return acceptance, tolerance, and love. This response is clearly seen, for example, in the longer story, "Franny," in which Zooey's sermon on the fat lady suggests this selfless way of encountering the world. I think then that Warren French is only partly correct when he insists that "One misleading thing about the story is that Teddy's palaver creates the feeling that mysticism is in some way involved in what happens" (*J. D. Salinger* 134). If we are misled into believing that Teddy himself is truly a mystic and clairvoyant, the story fails: it is incredible. But the ethic that Teddy derives from his acquaintance with Eastern religion stands in the story as a potential response to the difficulties of life in America. Teddy's doctrine of love is both defense and valid response to the crummy world. As such, it is a satisfactory conclusion to the *Nine Stories*, all of which dramatize the difficulties of "being born in an American body."

We must see, moreover, that Teddy's sense of not being loved, has produced in him an anger that is both expressed through and disguised by his pose of the junior savant. His response to the adult world is carefully controlled passive aggression, seen chiefly in his polite contempt for his parents and later the intrusive Nicholson. His obliquely expressed anger may be sensed, for example, in his response to Nicholson's inquiry about the education of children. Teddy, who equates "logic and intellectual stuff" with the fatal apple of Eden, responds: "I'd just make them vomit up every bit of the apple their parents and everybody made them take a bite out of" (106). The violent image of forcing small children to vomit up a kind of poison thrust upon them by the adult world suggests Teddy's anger and his sense that he and children generally are being poisoned by being brought up "in an American body."[3]

Like his spiritual kinsman, Seymour Glass of the collection's first story, whose importance to the later story I will discuss, Teddy, I would argue, commits suicide as the ultimate gesture of hostility and withdrawal, carefully planning it in advance to inspire terror and guilt. He deliberately designs his death so that the hateful Booper should be witness and victim, and her horror will later, of course, be shared by his miserable parents.

2

It is useful to approach Teddy through the first story in the collection: "A Perfect Day for Bananafish," since, I believe, *Nine Stories* reveals a thematic unity. The centrality of the character Seymour Glass to Salinger's fiction is well understood. Teddy and Seymour are closely related characters. Salinger called attention to the parallels between Teddy and Seymour in his introduction to *Seymour—An Introduction*, where, with irritating coyness, Salinger/Buddy says that some of the Glass family members thought that his description of Teddy's eyes looked very much like those of Seymour: "at least two members of my family knew and remarked that I was trying to get at his eyes with that description, [of Teddy's eyes] and even felt that I hadn't brought it off too badly, in a *peculiar* way" (132).[4] Surely a similarity of vision is suggested in the two characters. In Seymour the narrator, Buddy

Glass, a writer, says with wry amusement that some people tell him that all his stories are about one person only: Seymour.

"Teddy," the last story of the collection ends, as does the first story "A Perfect Day for Bananafish," with a suicide.[5] Seymour Glass kills himself sitting three feet away from the very embodiment of a world he cannot abide, his wife Muriel, and in a way that will cause the ultimate shock and horror. Teddy also kills himself in front of a female he intends to injure, that small concentration of hostility and meanness, his sister Booper, whose "all-piercing" scream can be thought of as an echo of the scream of Muriel a microsecond after the death of Seymour, and, of course, a forecast of the response of Teddy's own parents who will shortly learn of Teddy's death. The deeply disturbed Teddy throws himself into the empty pool (untouched by Booper) to protest and escape a life he cannot abide, and to inflict guilt feelings on his family and the adult world that has violated him through its ceaseless probing of his personality. Thus understood, there is no problematic ambiguity to the conclusion of "Teddy." Salinger's deliberate reduplication of the figure of Seymour from "Bananafish" in "Teddy" tells us exactly what happens at the end of Teddy's story. The motives of suicide are alike: to escape, protest, and inspire horror and guilt: in short, to punish the unloving, grown-up world in the person of a particularly dreadful female.[6]

We may say a little more about Seymour, then, and the crucial reflection of him in Teddy. We learn more of Seymour in the second of the *Nine Stories*, "Down at the Dingy," and outside the *Nine Stories* collection, most notably in *Raise High the Roof Beam, Carpenters, Seymour—An Introduction* and "Hapworth 16, 1924."[7] Like Teddy, Seymour is, we learn in *Carpenters*, careful and responsible concerning his family, suspicious of sentimentality (53), a connoisseur of *haiku*. He is a student of mysticism: like Teddy, he keeps a diary, and notes, "I've been reading a miscellany of Vedanta all day" (70). Another diary entry reflects a central fictional concern of Salinger—that of the care of children. Married couples are to "Raise their children honorably, lovingly, and with detachment. A child is a guest in the house, to be loved and respected—never possessed, since he belongs to god" (70). Thus Seymour's diary anticipates and glosses the story "Teddy."

As seen in the other stories in which he appears, Seymour Glass was as a child prodigy, the subject of examination by a hostile probing adult world, and this intense puzzlement about Seymour, seen both within the Glass family and the world outside the family, is ongoing. In "Bananafish," Seymour, obviously disturbed by his experience in the war, is the object of examination by all those who surround him—including the professional scrutiny of two psychiatrists named in the story. He is considered special, puzzling, something of a freak. The story begins with Mrs. Fedder, Muriel's mother, questioning Muriel about Seymour. We learn that Seymour is preoccupied with death: "Those horrible things he said to Granny about her plans for passing away" (6). His conversation with Sybil defies the "Western" logic that Teddy so discommends in his story. Intending to delight the girl, he refutes logic and reason with his witty, charming disregard for reality. He comments teasingly on Sybil's "yellow" bathing suit (actually blue) and his delight in fantasy is seen throughout their conversation. His story of the bananafish, freakish and self-destructive, defines his feelings about himself.

Like Teddy, Seymour, though on the point of suicide, is careful and responsible in his actions toward Sybil. But his hostility against the grown-up world (necessarily more suppressed in the much younger, dependent Teddy), emerges clearly: his anger toward the innocent woman in the elevator, whom he accuses of staring at his feet, reveals his hostility. Seymour projects a suicidal fantasy in the famous story of the bananafish, who, when trapped, die. At the end of the story, he kills himself. His death is an accusation: against the self-absorbed, non-understanding Muriel, against the adult world represented by her mother, Mrs. Fedder, and the psychiatrists—none of whom can understand or help him. Shooting himself while sitting close to the sleeping Muriel is the supremely hostile action, and one that he has planned in advance; he brought the gun with him to Florida.

Teddy, like Seymour, is a person of great potential at the time of his death. Like other unhappy Salinger kids in the collection, Teddy is detached from his parents, and from adults in general, secretive and withdrawn—though Teddy is seemingly the opposite: open, kind, careful, responsible. Teddy, far from being the serene little savant he seems, is in fact lonely, withdrawn, secretive, and emotionally dead, the angry victim of that "phony" adult world central to Salinger's fictional imagination. This situation, though disguised by Teddy's presentation of himself as kiddy-philosopher, is revealed in several key passages in the story and concludes in his horrific suicide.

As the story begins, Teddy is returning from Edinburgh and Oxford where he has been subject once again, as he has throughout his short life, to the puzzled examination of the academics. His curious adult-like poise, his obvious intelligence, seems to validate the sense of enlightened wisdom that he seems to embody. His life has been largely this examination; he is typically surrounded by questioning, baffled, sometimes amused, sometime hostile adults. To his examiners, he is a freak: "kidding around and asking me a bunch of questions ... they all kept sitting around smoking cigarettes and getting very kittenish" (192). Teddy is pleased to have some measure of comic revenge on these types: "I told them a little bit" about when they were fated to die. These scientists and academics are "phonies"—as much so as the various pedagogues in *Catcher in the Rye*. "I mean I knew that even though they teach Religion and Philosophy and all, they're still pretty afraid to die" (193). His parents, as we see in the brilliant opening scene, provide no counterbalance to this intrusive, careless world: the negligence and indeed hostility of the parents are fatal.

The first scene is set in the small stateroom of Teddy's parents. Salinger dramatizes with skill and economy the inadequacy of Teddy's parents. They are at odds: tension and hostility permeate the atmosphere as the parents lie abed late, irritable and languorous, presumably hungover after a long smoky, boozy night. The father is presented as an unpleasant failure: an impostor as a man, with his "third-class leading man's speaking voice: narcissistically deep and resonant, functionally prepared at a moment's notice to out-male anyone in the same room with it, if necessary even a small boy" (167). His voice is "theatrical" and an element of competition with his own son is suggested. His irritable carping ("I'll exquisite day you, buddy"), his incessant and slovenly smoking and whining low-grade sarcasm all suggest the weak, the unmanly. This sense is heightened by the image of his "nude, inflamed-pink, right arm" (155), flicking ashes from the cigarette. The suggestion is of the anger of this narcissistic showbiz failure—anger, prompted by jealousy of his own son— and of sickness, even degeneracy. Mrs. McArdle's hostility toward her failure of a husband is not disguised; it is expressed through her saccharin, hostile wit. Teddy's farewell kiss is unwilling and perfunctory—as she "brought her left arm out from under the sheet, as if bent on encircling Teddy's waist with it" (172), he slides away. Her hostility toward her husband is expressed in her phony display of affection for Teddy, syrupy, and suggestive of the lazily sexual and perverse. The sheet drawn "tight over her very probably nude body" (168), the anger between these two unpleasant types flares out: near the end of the scene, Mr. McArdle snarls at his wife, "I'd like to kick your goddamn head open" (168), followed by his wife's sarcastically sweet hopes for his heart attack and a funeral where she would sit as a widow dressed in scarlet in the first row, attracting male attention.

Teddy's response to this is withdrawal and passive aggression. He is detached, unhearing. The phrase, "Teddy, did you hear me," is repeated; but, pointedly, he does not respond. What is ominous here is Teddy's recurring hints concerning his own death, implicit in his suggestions that once out of sight, entities (orange peels in this case) would not exist, and culminating in "After I go out this door, I may only exist in the minds of all my acquaintances" (173–74). The section ends, "He closed the door behind him" (174). And thus he closes out his life with his estranged parents.

Brother-sister relations are important in Salinger and here, although it may seem that Teddy and Booper are entirely different, I suggest Booper mirrors and thus makes clear the anger and preoccupation with death that is Teddy's psychological center. Her essence is anger, hostility, and aggression, and obviously this stems from the McArdle family situation—plus of course her jealously toward her celebrity brother. She echoes her parents' anger on a smaller scale, and she shares her mother's penchant for aggressive fantasy. She vents her anger on the hapless little boy Myron; images of death run throughout her conversation, expressing hostility toward her own parents, albeit in a disguised form. If Myron's mother dies he will be an orphan; two "giants" could throw shuffleboard disks at the passengers and kill them; they could kill Myron's parents—and "if that didn't kill them, you know what you could do? You could put some poison on some marshmallows and make them eat it" (177). As she leaves for the pool for her lesson, she once again expresses her all-consuming anger: "I hate you! I hate everybody in this ocean!" (178).

Teddy, despite his seeming tranquillity, shares this anger and his death, suicide, is a last hostile gesture, directed primarily at his parents, sister, and the rest of the prying and hostile adult world in which he feels alone and isolated. His barely disguised anger emerges in his carefully polite indifference to his parents, to Nicholson, and even in the short scenes in which he dismisses the stewardess and purser. The source of this anger is revealed when he tells Nicholson of his parents: "They don't love me and Booper—that's my sister. . . . I mean they don't seem able to love us just the way we are. They don't seem able to love us unless they can keep changing us a little bit. They love their reasons for loving us almost as much as they love us, and most of the time more" (187).

Along with anger, his feeling of isolation is the another cause of his suicide, as suggested by his recitation of the *haiku*: "Along this road goes no one, this autumn eve" (185). Seymour too writes a *haiku* shortly before his death. Teddy's feelings of being alienated from his parents and the world, his superior intelligence, his fear of and his impatience with the probing examiners leave him with no one to talk to. Teddy is unwilling to speak openly or intimately to any of the adults—most especially the stranger Nicholson whose intrusive questions Teddy seeks to avoid.

Intermingled with this sense of isolation is his emotional deadness, his fear and rejection of the feelings. He insists on this strongly everywhere—associating it, contemptuously, with poetry and sentiment. To Nicholson:

I wish I knew why people think it's so important to be emotional. . . . My mother and father don't think a person's human unless he thinks a lot of things are very sad or very annoying or very—very unjust, sort of. My father gets very emotional even when he reads the newspaper. He thinks I'm inhuman. (186)

His reaction to his egoistic and irresponsible parents has been withdrawal, a suppression of anger and the deadening of his emotions. For Teddy, emotions are disturbing; the anger he feels must not be expressed. This becomes clear in a key diary entry—a self revealing fantasy, just as Seymour's fantasy of the Bananafish and Gedsudski's Laughing Man reveal their most significant inner feelings. After reminding himself to ask Professor Mandell not to send any more poetry books—those compilations of emotion and sentimentality—Teddy fantasizes:

> A man walks along the beach and unfortunately gets hit in the head by a coconut. His head unfortunately creaks open in two halves. Then his wife comes along the beach singing a song and sees the halves and recognizes them and picks them up. She gets very sad of course and cries heart-breakingly. That is exactly where I am tired of poetry. Supposing the lady just picks up the 2 halves and shouts into them very angrily, 'stop that!' (180)

The implications of this fantasy in regard to his own parents are suggestive: the husband is killed violently, in a farcical, cartoon fashion; the wife previously happy, becomes very sad when she recognizes what has happened, and cries heartbreakingly. The unfortunate man involved in this farcical fantasy is both Mr. McArdle, victim of his son's hostile fantasy, and Teddy himself, eliciting the grief and guilt he desires from his mother.

His last diary entry, October 28, 1952, reveals no significant plans for future action. Indeed, the nine letters written in the morning have a farewell quality, and the previous day's memo to look up the phrase "gift horse," becomes in the next and final day, the observation "Life is a gift horse in my opinion": that is, life is seemingly delightful and amazing; actually deadly. His final entry, "It will either happen today or February 14, 1958" (182), seems to suggest ongoing deliberation about suicide.

That Teddy targets Valentine's Day, with its suggestions of erotic love, as an appropriate day for his suicide suggests that another uneasiness disturbs the preadolescent Teddy and indeed helps to trigger his decision to end his life this day and not six years later. He feels anxiety concerning his new and disturbing awareness of sex. This is seen in his awareness of his mother's nude form, encircling arm, and attempted kiss, Ensign Matthewson's lipsticky mouth, the casual brush of the stewardess's hand (a huge, blond woman), against his hair. This sexual anxiety is further clarified by Teddy's fanciful notion that in a previous life his spiritual development was going very well indeed, until sexuality entered in. His spiritual advancement was abruptly halted when "I met a lady and I sort of stopped meditating" (188). Typically of such Salinger figures, he qualifies and digresses—but there was a fall: "I wouldn't have had to get incarnated in an American body if I hadn't met that lady" (188).

Teddy's unease with his incipient sexuality is also projected in his reference to the Adam and Eve story in conversation with Nicholson. The myth that the apple transferred fatal knowledge to mankind has sometimes been understood in terms of sexuality, particularly as the story contains a seduction that leads to sexual shame and exclusion from paradise. In this pointed reference to the biblical story, one recognizes a preoccupation within Salinger's fiction at work. Critics have repeatedly noted that throughout Salinger there is a distrust, an uneasiness, with sexuality. Sex sullies and spoils. A sense of covert sexuality can be seen in Seymour Glass's relationship with the girl, Sybil. Seymour, apparently uneasy with mature sexual relations, seeks out the child, Sybil, and his encounter with her is latently sexual.[8] When he returns to the hotel, to the inevitable intimacy of his relationship with Muriel, he ends his life.

It is this new, uneasy sexual awareness that advances his decision to die immediately. He says to Nicholson:

> "For example, I have a swimming lesson in about five minutes, I could go downstairs to the pool, and there might not be any water in it. . . . I might walk up to the edge of it, just to have a look at the bottom, for instance and my sister might come up and sort of push me in. I could fracture my skull and die instantaneously. . . . That could happen, all right." (193)

His death is considered, long incubating. It is triggered by the perversity and hostility of his parents, a fresh demonstration of Booper's willfulness and anger, his disturbing awareness of his new sexuality, and yet another endless interrogation by a foolish and insensitive academic phony. That Teddy somehow does not know that there is in fact no water in the pool, that this is cleaning day, is impossible: surely this careful reader of the ship's bulletins realizes this and yet he makes an appointment to meet Booper at 10:30 and reminds her repeatedly and urgently of this appointment. It is clearly his intention to deliberately kill himself by jumping into the empty pool in front of his sister, parallel to Seymour's shocking death next to that person who most directly represents what he most despises and loathes, Miss Spiritual Tramp of 1958. The scream of course is Booper's—it is the first sign of the horror and guilt that Teddy has intentionally inflicted upon his loathsome family and the adult world more generally. It is interesting that in both "Bananafish" and "Teddy" Salinger inserts a suspenseful uncertainty. In the first story, the reader does not know what is going to happen until the last three words: until then Seymour's anger may lead him to destroy himself or Miss Spiritual Tramp.[9] In "Teddy," the ambiguity is more radical; yet the murder of Booper (as some readers have thought it) would make no fictional sense in context, and the signals of Teddy's approaching suicide are too strong.

3

The story "Teddy" concludes *Nine Stories* by dramatizing a potential answer to the corruption, materiality, egotism, and self-seeking of American life: individual rejection of the Western culture and the attempt to gain a truer understanding and fuller humanity through renunciation of the self and unqualified love of a very imperfect human race. Between "Teddy" and "Bananafish" are contrasting stories of redemption. We recognize the sudden understanding of human difficulty experienced by Ginnie Mannox in "Just before the War with the Eskimos," and the patient, sensitive love of a parent, Boo Boo Tannenbaum, for her highly susceptible and anxious son in "Down at the Dinghy." A gesture of human affinity, the gift by Esmé of her father's watch, thus selecting Sergeant X as her surrogate—at long distance—father, is cathartic for the man in despair. In "De Daumier-Smith's Blue Period," the troubled adolescent is saved and returned to sanity by a realization of the purity of Sister Irma and a sudden comic glimpse of Eden in the midst of an image of human despair.

It is ironic and tragic that this gift of love, as mediated though a figure like Esmé, Boo Boo, or Sister Irma, is unavailable to Teddy even though he insists on the possibility of redemption through love. He can feel in himself no power of forgiveness and tolerance through redemptive love. Unlike his literary relation Franny, he has no Zooey to mediate between his feelings of anger and despair, and the love he seeks. A frightened, loveless child, Teddy attempts to maintain his defensive posture as little savant, but finally even this extraordinary persona fails him. Like Seymour, fear and anger overwhelm him.

That Salinger's advocates of this doctrine of redemptive love, Seymour and Teddy, both take their own lives in unexpected and shocking manner irrevocably compromises the positive thematic implications of the collection. Universal love may be an ideal, but very possibly it is impossible to achieve when one is imprisoned "in an American body."

The significance of "Teddy" to the rest of *Nine Stories* is clear. Teddy's doctrine offers a potential solution, if a problematic one, to the problem of being born in an American body. We see that what Teddy claims he has done (rejected the materialism and egotism of American life) is exactly what must be done, according to Salinger, and this possibility is seen again in certain other stories of the collection. Yet "Teddy" closes the collection on a note of failure forecast in the opening story: the possibility of redemptive love is fleeting and in most cases, ungraspable. Without the mediation of healing love, Teddy, Seymour and their kind are isolated and doomed: "Along this road goes no one, this autumn eve."

NOTES

1. Frederick L. Gwynn and Joseph L. Blotner note the "growing diffuseness of the story and the ambiguity of the conclusion" (40). James Lundquist complains of inadequate characterization and the weakness of the dialogue between Teddy and Nicholson and: " . . . the major thing wrong with the story is that it does not move. Its static quality is the consequence of contrast without conflict" (108). Paul Kirschner concludes that the story " . . . seems no more than the tantalizing adumbration of a religious philosophy" (75). Laurence Perrine concludes that while Teddy is "a vivid and brilliantly written story . . . its focus is uncertain and its conclusion mystifying." Perrine maintains that the ambiguity of the conclusion "suggests that the author either was unclear in his aims or lacked the courage of his conviction" (223).

2. French suggests that "Teddy's attitude" . . . may also be an extremely bright and hypersensitive young person's rationalization of his desire to escape from what he finds an intolerable situation" (*Revisited* 85). But I certainly disagree with French's insistence that Teddy is a cunning little hypocrite, with a shrewdly calculating nature. French finds Teddy "one of the most obnoxious puppets in the whole history of bratty children" (*Revisited* 133). I suggest that his whole presentation of himself as a mystic and clairvoyant is his intuitive, defensive response to an intolerable situation. It is significant that nobody in the story is entirely convinced of his authenticity as mystic and clairvoyant. His professional examiners in Oxford and Boston are impressed, but not entirely convinced. They are puzzled, annoyed, disturbed, and so on.

3. Teddy's dreadful little sister Booper, his mirror and foil, speaks gleefully of poisoning: "You could put some poison on some marshmallows and make them eat it" (177).

4. Teddy's eyes are "slightly crossed," surely Salinger's hint, evoking as it does the term cock-eyed, the ersatz quality of Teddy's powers as mystic and clairvoyant.

5. T. L. Gross (263) points out the centrality of suicide to Salinger's fiction. "The act of suicide—at times it seems the only act in all of Salinger's fiction—occurs . . . when Salinger first begins to write with a clarity of focus and with real efficacy. . . ."

6. Thomas Kranidas insists that Teddy's suicide is not tragic, since it is the decision of an enlightened ("immortally composed") person to leave an unsatisfactory existence. "There ought not to be worry over the death of Teddy, whose very message was transcendence" (91). I argue of course that the story is primarily a psychological study of a child who reacts to his difficult situation by claiming to possess authentic mysticism and supernatural powers. He is certainly not a conscious hypocrite. Instead he consciously believes in what he announces to the world.

7. James Bryan notes the similarity of Seymour in "Hapworth" to Teddy. Both are incredibly precocious and also disturbed by incipient sexuality (357).

8. In "Raise High the Roof Beam, Carpenters," Seymour fails to appear at his own wedding. In "Bananafish," the sexual desire he feels for the girl Sybil emerges when, to her consternation, he grasps and kisses her foot.

9. Earlier in "Bananafish" there is considerable uncertainty as to Seymour's intentions to the little girl, Sybil. He pushes her farther and farther out to sea and she grows frightened. Is he going to drown her? Seymour's obvious mental disorder leads the reader to feel anxiety as to his intentions, especially as we recall the highly ambiguous kissing of the little girl's foot as he pushes her out to deeper waters.

WORKS CITED

Bryan, James. "A Reading of Salinger's 'Teddy.'" *American Literature* 40 (1968): 352–69.

French, Warren. *J. D. Salinger*. Rev. ed. Boston: Twayne, 1963.

———. *J. D. Salinger Revisited*. Boston: Twayne, 1988.

Galloway, David D. "The Love Ethic." *J. D. Salinger*. Ed. Harold Bloom. *Modern Critical Views*. New York: Chelsea, 1987. 29–51.

Goldstein, Bernice, and Sanford Goldstein. "Zen and Salinger." *Modern Fiction Studies* 12 (1966): 313–324.

Gross, T. L. "J. D. Salinger: Suicide and Survival in the Modern World." *The Heroic Ideal in American Literature*. New York: Free Press, 1971. 262–71.

Gwynn, Frederick L. and Joseph L. Blotner. *The Fiction of J. D. Salinger*. Pittsburgh: U of Pittsburgh P, 1958.

Kirschner, Paul. "Salinger and his Society: The Pattern of *Nine Stories*." *Literary Half-Yearly* 14 (1969–70; rpt. 1973): 63–78.

Kranidas, Thomas. "Point of View in Salinger's 'Teddy.'" *Studies in Short Fiction* 2 (1964): 89–91.

Lundquist, James. *J. D. Salinger*. New York: Ungar, 1979.

Perrine, Laurence. "Teddy? Booper? Or Blooper?" *Studies in Short Fiction* 4 (1967): 217–24.

Salinger, J. D. *Nine Stories*. New York: Bantam, 1964.

———. *Raise High the Roof Beam* and *Seymour—An Introduction*. London: Penguin, 1963.

Stein, William Bysshe. "Salinger's 'Teddy': *Tat Tvam Asi* or That Thou Art." *Arizona Quarterly* 29 (1973): 253–56.

EBERHARD ALSEN

New Light on the Nervous Breakdowns of Salinger's Sergeant X and Seymour Glass

In her memoir *Dream Catcher* (2000), J. D. Salinger's daughter Margaret reveals some hitherto unknown information that sheds new light on J. D. Salinger's nervous breakdown at the end of World War II and on the nervous breakdowns of two of Salinger's fictional characters, Sergeant X in "For Esmé—with Love and Squalor" and ex-sergeant Seymour Glass in "A Perfect Day for Bananafish." Remembering conversations with her father about World War II, Margaret Salinger says: "As a counter intelligence officer my father was one of the first soldiers to walk into a certain, just liberated, concentration camp. He told me the name, but I no longer remember." She also quotes her father as saying, "You never really get the smell of burning flesh out of your nostrils, no matter how long you live."[1]

* * *

We know about Salinger's nervous breakdown from a letter that he wrote to Ernest Hemingway from Germany in 1945 (The two had met twice during the war). In this undated letter, Salinger writes that he has checked himself into "a General Hospital in Nürnberg" because he has been in "an almost constant state of despondency." Two references in the letter suggest that it must have been written in May or June of 1945. Salinger mentions that a

---

From *CLA Journal* 45, no. 3 (March 2002): 379–87. Copyright © 2002 by the College Language Association.

few arrests are still left to be made in his CIC section, and he also mentions that the commanding officer of his CIC detachment, Captain Appleton, has returned to the United States before the rest of the regiment. Salinger's regiment was shipped home on July 3, 1945.[2]

Salinger tries to downplay his nervous breakdown, and he makes fun of the psychiatrists asking him about his sex life and his childhood. However, he also expresses his fear that he may receive a psychiatric discharge from the Army. This suggests that his case must have been fairly severe (the Hemingway letter can be examined in the Princeton University Library).

Several biographers have assumed that Salinger's nervous breakdown was due to "combat fatigue" (traumatic stress disorder). For instance, Salinger's daughter Margaret notes that her father's regiment was involved in some of the bloodiest battles of World War II, from the D-Day invasion through the battles of Cherbourg, Mortain, and the Hürtgen Forest, all the way to the Battle of the Bulge. And indeed, Colonel Gerden F. Johnson, one of the battalion commanders in Salinger's regiment, reports that during the Battle of Mortain in northern France, the carnage was so frightful that "there were many cases of combat fatigue even among our older men" (Johnson 163). But that was in July of 1944, and Salinger had his nervous breakdown in May of 1945, shortly after the end of the war.

It is unlikely that Salinger's nervous breakdown was due to "combat fatigue" because he was not a combat infantryman but a member of the Counter Intelligence Corps. Counter intelligence operatives were attached to division and battalion headquarters companies whose command posts were usually located quite a distance behind the lines. As a counter intelligence sergeant, Salinger had the task of interviewing prisoners of war and civilians in order to find out information about enemy troop strength, number of tanks, location of heavy artillery, supply depots, and so forth. He had a jeep at his disposal in order to quickly get to places where prisoners had been taken or where a village had been liberated. It is therefore safe to assume that Sergeant Salinger's nervous breakdown was not due to the stress of combat. It is more likely that it was due to what he witnessed at the concentration camp that he mentioned to his daughter.

That camp was probably the one near the village of Hurlach, Bavaria. It was discovered on April 27, 1945, by elements of the 493rd Field Artillery Battalion of the 12th Armored Division.[3] Salinger could easily have gotten to the camp, if not on the day it was first discovered, then on one of the next two days, because on April 27, the command post of Salinger's regiment was in the village of Agawang, seventeen miles northwest of Hurlach, and two days later it was in the village of Winkl, only nine miles east of the camp (Johnson 391).

The Hurlach concentration camp was officially called "Kaufering Lager IV." It was one of the eleven small camps of the Kaufering complex that was named after the small town seven miles north of Landsberg, where the first of the eleven camps was built. The over 22,000 prisoners in the Kaufering camps were mostly Jewish slave laborers from Poland, France, Hungary, and many other countries that had been overrun by the Nazis. These slave laborers were employed in building an underground aircraft factory that the Nazis had code-named "Ringeltaube" (wood pigeon). This factory was to consist of three gigantic, domed bunkers in which the jet fighter Messerschmitt 262 was to be produced at a rate of 900 planes a month. By the end of the war, the construction of two of the bunkers had been abandoned, and the construction of the third was about 70 percent completed.[4]

Kaufering Lager IV near Hurlach was an extermination camp. It was designated as the "Krankenlager" for the other Kaufering camps, but that name was a cynical euphemism because the sick prisoners received no medical attention and were simply allowed to die from their illnesses or from starvation. Between 4,000 to 5,000 prisoners died in the camp from the time the camp was opened in June 1944 and the time it was occupied by American troops in April 1945. American soldiers later found these bodies in two nearby mass graves. On the day before the Americans arrived, the SS guards evacuated some 3,000 prisoners by train and killed all those who were too weak or too sick to travel. The SS guards fled only four hours before the first GIs discovered the camp.[5]

In addition to being the only extermination camp in the Kaufering complex (the other ten were work camps), the Hurlach camp also has the distinction of being the only camp that the SS set on fire before they left it. Lt. Colonel Edward F. Seiller of the 12th Armored Division explains: "When one of our infantry battalions approached Kaufering Lager No. 4, someone at the camp (presumably the SS guards), herded the inmates into the barracks, nailed the doors shut, and set the barracks on fire."[6] Sergeant Robert T. Hartwig remembers that when he and another GI approached Hurlach in their jeep, they "knew [they] were near a camp because of the sickening odor of burning bodies";[7] and Corporal Pete Bramble reports that "the stench was terrible, especially the burning corpses."[8] This is also what Salinger remembers most about the camp.

The sights at the Hurlach camp were no less gruesome than the smell. In addition to 268 burned corpses, the GIs found close to a hundred bodies scattered over the camp, along a path to the railroad tracks, and in a nearby forest. Photos taken by Sergeant Hartwig, Corporal Bramble, and other American soldiers show that the corpses were literally only skin and bones, and some probably weighed no more than 50 to 70 pounds. These horrifying photos can be found in Ken Bradstreet's combat history of the Twelfth Armored Division, entitled *Hellcats*, on the web site entitled *The Twelfth Armored Division and the Liberation of Death Camps*, and on the web site of the Simon Wiesenthal Multimedia Learning Center. Some of the photos show blackened bodies still smoldering in the ruins of the burned-down barracks. These pictures support the assumption that it was indeed at Hurlach that Salinger encountered the smell of burning flesh, which he said he would never be able to get out of his nostrils.

Salinger's response to what he witnessed at the concentration camp shows up only indirectly in his fiction. "A Girl I Knew" (1948) is the only story in which Salinger mentions the concentration camps. In that story, a CIC sergeant interviews civilians and prisoners of war in order to ferret out members of the SS, who not only committed atrocities at the concentration camps but were also infamous for massacres such as the shooting of 81 American prisoners of war during the Battle of the Bulge near Malmedy, Belgium. Aside from hunting for disguised SS-men, Salinger's narrator also has a personal agenda: Whenever he comes across Austrians, he asks them whether they know what happened to a Jewish girl from Vienna whom he knew before the war. He eventually learns from a Jewish doctor who had just returned from the Buchenwald concentration camp that the girl and her family "were burned to death in an incinerator."[9]

Even though Salinger mentions nothing in his fiction about what he saw and smelled at the Hurlach concentration camp, the effect of this experience shows up in two stories. Like Sergeant Salinger, both Sergeant X in "For Esmé—with Love and Squalor" and ex-sergeant Seymour Glass in "A Perfect Day for Bananafish" served in the European Theater of Operations and suffered nervous breakdowns. But in both stories we are shown only the symptoms of their nervous breakdowns and must guess what the causes were. The two stories take on a new dimension if we assume that Sergeant X and Sergeant Seymour Glass shared Sergeant Salinger's concentration camp experience.

"For Esmé—with Love and Squalor" (1950) is Salinger's most autobiographical story. It deals with the nervous breakdown of an unnamed Counter Intelligence sergeant at the end of World War II. At the beginning of the story, Sergeant X is being trained for the D-Day invasion at an Army base in a small town in the South of England. That town is modeled after Tiverton in Devonshire, where Sergeant Salinger himself was trained by the CIC. At the end of the war, Sergeant X is part of the army of occupation and is stationed in Gaufurt, Bavaria, the fictitious counterpart of the town of Weiszenburg, south of Nürnberg, where Salinger interviewed Nazi civilians.[10]

Sergeant X's nervous breakdown is the main topic in "For Esmé—with Love and Squalor," but we do not find out what caused it, because the story skips from a few days before the D-Day invasion to a time "several weeks after V-E Day (Victory in Europe, May 7, 1945)."[11] Sergeant X has just returned from a two-weeks' stay at an Army hospital in Frankfurt, Germany, where he has been treated for what the narrator calls a "nervous breakdown" rather than "combat fatigue" ("Esmé" ["For Esmé—with Love and Squalor"] 109). Whatever treatment Sergeant X received at the hospital did not help much because upon his return he says that he still feels as if his mind were about "to dislodge itself and teeter, like insecure luggage on an overhead rack" ("Esmé" 104). Moreover, he feels so nauseous most of the time that he keeps a wastebasket handy into which to vomit; also, his jeep driver, Corporal Clay, tells him, "[T]he goddam side of your face is jumping all over the place" ("Esmé" 109); and finally, the sergeant's hands shake so much that when he tries to write, his writing is "almost entirely illegible" ("Esmé" 105).

It is most likely that in describing the aftereffects of Sergeant X's nervous breakdown, Salinger was drawing on his personal experience. In his letter to Hemingway, he does not mention any of his symptoms except his "almost constant state of despondency." However, there is definite evidence that he shared at least one of Sergeant X's afflictions, namely the uncontrollable trembling of his hands. Salinger's daughter Margaret examined the letters that her father wrote during the spring and summer of 1945 and reports that his handwriting became "something totally unrecognizable" (*Dream Catcher* 68).

The nervous breakdowns of Sergeant Salinger and Sergeant X illuminate one another. "For Esmé—with Love and Squalor" illustrates the aftereffects of the nervous collapse, the feeling of vertigo, the nausea, the facial tic, and the trembling hands, and Salinger's visit to a concentration camp suggests that the cause of his and Sergeant X's nervous breakdowns was not the stress of battle but the atrocities they witnessed during the last days of the war.

Salinger's concentration camp experience also sheds new light on the suicide of Seymour Glass, the central character in "A Perfect Day for Bananafish" and "Seymour—An Introduction." In "Seymour—An Introduction," we learn that like Salinger, Seymour was also a sergeant in the Army,[12] also served in the European Theater of Operations, and also wound up in Germany at the end of the war ("Seymour" ["Seymour—An Introduction"] 113). Moreover, in "A Perfect Day for Bananafish," a psychiatrist says about Seymour that "it was a perfect crime that the Army released him from the hospital" because "there's a very great chance that Seymour may completely lose control of himself."[13] This comment suggests that Seymour was a patient in a psychiatric ward of an Army hospital.

No one who has written about the suicide of Seymour Glass has commented on the significance of the unusual length of time—almost three years—that he spent in an Army hospital. He killed himself on March 18, 1948,[14] and Buddy mentions that Seymour returned from Germany on a commercial flight "a week or so" before his suicide ("Seymour" 134). That means Seymour did not come home to the United States until almost three years after the end of the war. Moreover, Buddy also says that Seymour spent "the last three years of his life both in and out of the Army, but mostly in, well in" ("Seymour" 114). In short, Seymour's mental illness was so severe that the Army psychiatrists did not simply release him with a psychiatric discharge—which is something that almost happened to Salinger—but they decided to keep him "well in," that is, locked up in a psychiatric ward for close to three years.

Seymour's extended stay in an Army hospital raises the question of what it was that caused his nervous breakdown and mental illness. Unless we assume that Seymour and Sergeant X are the same person (which some critics have done), there is no information in Salinger's fiction so far about Seymour's war experiences. Seymour may have been a combat infantryman, and he may have been severely wounded. Or he may have been one of the few survivors of a massacre such as the one at Malmedy. But since none of this happened to Salinger, it makes more sense to assume that Seymour's nervous breakdown—like Salinger's—was not caused by "combat fatigue" but by the horrifying sights and smells of one of the many concentration camps.

*   *   *

There is a chance that we may still find out whether it was indeed their concentration camp experiences that explain why Sergeant X had a nervous breakdown and why ex-sergeant Seymour Glass became so despondent that he eventually killed himself. Although Salinger has said on more than one occasion that he does not plan to publish anymore during his lifetime (for instance in his phone call to *New York Times* reporter Lacey Fosburgh), his daughter Margaret said in a National Public Radio interview that her father "is writing every day," that "he is planning to publish after his death," and that he has "a large number of stories ready to go."[15]

NOTES

1. Margaret Salinger, *Dream Catcher* (New York: Washington Square, 2000) 55. Hereafter cited parenthetically in the text.

2. Colonel Gerden F. Johnson, *History of the Twelfth Infantry Regiment in World War II* (Boston: Twelfth Infantry Regiment, 1947) 391. Hereafter cited parenthetically in the text.

3. Ken Bradstreet, ed., *Hellcats* [WW II Combat History of the Twelfth Armored Division] (Paducah, KY: Turner, 1987) 117–19.

4. Anton Posset, "Deckname Ringeltaube," *Themenhefte Landsberger Zeitgeschichte* 4 (1993): 18–24.

5. Anton Posset, "Die amerikanische Armee entdeckt den Holocaust," *Themenhefte Landsberger Zeitgeschichte* 2 (1993): 41.

6. Colonel Edward Seiller, "Edward F. Seiller, 12th Armored Division," *The Twelfth Armored Division and the Liberation of Death Camps*, 1. <http://www.acu.edu/academics/history/12ad/cmpsx/seiller.htm>.

7. Bradstreet 118.

8. Corporal A. G. Bramble, "A. G. 'Pete' Bramble, 12th Armored Division," *The Twelfth Armored Division and the Liberation of the Death Camps*, 1. <http://www.acu.edu/academics/history/12ad/campsx/bramble.htm>.

9. J. D. Salinger, "A Girl I Knew," *Good Housekeeping* 128 (Feb. 1948): 196.

10. J. D. Salinger, Letter to Ernest Hemingway, Carlos Baker Collection of Ernest Hemingway (Princeton, NJ: Princeton U Library, n.d.).

11. J. D. Salinger, "For Esmé—with Love and Squalor," in *Nine Stories* [1953] (New York: Bantam, 1964) 103. Hereafter cited parenthetically in the text.

12. J. D. Salinger, *Raise High the Roof Beam, Carpenters; and Seymour—An Introduction* [1963] (New York: Bantam, 1965) 171. Hereafter cited parenthetically in the text.

13. J. D. Salinger, "A Perfect Day for Bananafish," in *Nine Stories* [1953] (New York: Bantam, 1964) 6.

14. J. D. Salinger, *Franny and Zooey* [1961] (New York: 1964) 62.

15. Margaret Salinger, "Margaret Salinger on J. D. Salinger," *The Connection*, National Public Radio, WBUR, Boston 14 Sept. 2000. <http://www.theconnection.org/archive/2000/09/0914b.shtml>.

DOMINIC SMITH

Salinger's Nine Stories: *Fifty Years Later*

Fifty years ago, J. D. Salinger published *Nine Stories*, his second book and arguably the highpoint of his foreshortened publishing career. *Nine Stories* was the best-selling collection that introduced and killed Seymour Glass— the brooding figure that gave rise to the Glass family dynasty, the fictional subject that held Salinger's attention until he stopped publishing in 1965. It was with this book that Salinger's art and life intersected best, where his Zen interests coalesced with his emerging themes, where he gave new life to the American short story. Not since Hemingway's *In Our Time* had a collection of stories so raised the bar on the form, creating characters and scenes that were hypnotic, mysterious, and unusually powerful.

Nineteen fifty-three was a year of bravado and dramatic change: Eisenhower was elected president, Stalin died, and Edmund Hillary conquered Everest. American magazines were full of advertisements for electronic transistors dubbed the "Little Giants," and Orville Wright published an essay in *Harper's* called "How We Invented the Airplane." The national mood combined post-war optimism with a cavalier belief in technology. But there was also an undercurrent of despair, a sense of entering a turbulent era. Thornton Wilder published a magazine piece on the declining moral standards of America's youth, and John Cheever, as if to chronicle these uncertain times, published *The Enormous Radio and Other Stories*—featuring such emblematic

From *Antioch Review* 61, no. 4 (Fall 2003): 639–49. Copyright © 2003 by Dominic Smith.

titles as "The Season of Divorce," "O City of Broken Dreams," and "Christmas is a Sad Season for the Poor."

Nine Stories tapped into this ambivalent milieu: the stories dealt with genius, spiritual integrity, moral corruption, and the occasional ability of innocence to transform our lives. If there was social angst over the morality of America's youth then Salinger couldn't have disagreed more—seven of the nine stories feature children, all of whom stand on higher moral ground than their adult guardians.

Salinger was thirty-four when *Nine Stories* came out and already a national literary figure, largely due to the popularity of his first book, *The Catcher in the Rye* (1951). But even at this early stage of success, Salinger was uneasy with fame, refusing interviews and dodging the press. Those who were allowed into his social circle described him as aloof and wry, as having a "dark aura" and "an incredibly strong physical and mental presence." The Hemingway biographer A. E. Hotchner described Salinger from around this time as having "an ego of cast iron" and confesses, "I found his intellectual flailings enormously attractive, peppered as they were with sardonic wit and a myopic sense of humor." In 1953 Salinger was a World War II veteran, he'd been married and divorced, he was darkly disillusioned, but he was also a rising star in American letters. Like the era itself, he was a mixed bag.

Thematically, *Nine Stories* landed somewhere between hope and despair, between what Salinger termed "love and squalor." Often, these two extremes are combined within the same story—the edginess of Seymour Glass in "A Perfect Day for Bananafish" coupled with his childlike innocence; the spiritual wisdom of the boy genius in "Teddy" as he plods toward his own unpleasant fate; the drunken self-indulgence of the mother in "Uncle Wiggily in Connecticut" combined with the daughter's endearing imaginary world; the pleasure of hearing boyhood stories involving Chinese bandits and emerald vaults in the Black Sea in "The Laughing Man" juxtaposed with the betrayal of the storyteller. But the flagship story for this contrast is "For Esmé—with Love and Squalor," which portrays an American army sergeant who finds redemption in a gift from a young British girl. In the wake of V-E Day the soldier has suffered a nervous breakdown. Unable to sleep but deeply fatigued, he receives a package from Esmé, whom he'd met briefly in an English teashop. Inside the package is Esmé's watch, once belonging to her father who was killed in action. The sergeant, so moved by the gift, begins to ascend from his battlefield trauma. "Then, suddenly, almost ecstatically, he felt sleepy. You take a really sleepy man, Esmé, and he always stands a chance of again becoming a man with all his fac—with all his f-a-c-u-l-t-i-e-s intact."

The damage and cost of war echoes in other stories as well. In "Just Before the War with the Eskimos," a jaded young man who worked in a warplane factory sees everything in terms of the next campaign—he's half-convinced that the "goddam fools" in the streets are waiting to be drafted to fight the Eskimos. Seymour Glass is a war victim recently discharged from a military mental ward. His brother, Walter, is the dead and lamented soldier in "Uncle Wiggily in Connecticut," a man killed by a freak wartime accident in the Pacific. This is the first and last time Salinger draws so directly from his experiences of war.

The thematic concerns of the stories are supported by an abundance of technical skill. The intensity of observation, the precision of language, the creation of meaning through the juxtaposition of scene, the ironic, razor-sharp dialogue, all suggest an artist working at the height of his craft. There is also a dogged faith in the dramatic moment and a strong controlling intention. But the stories derive meaning without ever sacrificing the mystery of human experience; they try to suggest more than they try to illustrate and in this way remain illusive at their core.

But if *Nine Stories* tapped into the buried ambivalence of the fifties, it also defied the social and artistic climate of the time. In lieu of the customary author photo—which Salinger had refused since the third print run of *The Catcher in the Rye*—was a Zen koan: *We know the sound of two hands clapping. But what is the sound of one hand clapping?* A koan has no right answer; it's designed to float in the mind of the Zen aspirant. While the riddle may be approached from all sides, often over the course of many years, the essence of the conundrum remains insoluble. This seems to mirror Salinger's mission with *Nine Stories*: to create engaging paradoxes or puzzles that, at their core, both reflect life yet refuse to be a part of it. The stories set out to illuminate characters but have their actions remain slightly beyond our grasp, to create what Flannery O'Connor once called the "mystery of personality."

* * *

The Catcher in the Rye had already earned Salinger critical praise and a wide readership from college professors, to high school students, to supermarket book buyers. Within a short time it was on the required reading lists at hundreds of colleges and universities around the country, and it sold in the U.S. at the steady clip of 250,000 copies a year. But it would be a mistake to assume that *Nine Stories* rode on the coattails of *Catcher's* popularity. They were both successful in their own right and for different reasons. The novel, in the tradition of *The Adventures of Huckleberry Finn*, contained an intoxicating blend of pathos and humor, a deep sense of irony, and a cadenced, colloquial voice. It was a masterly satire of the East Coast prep-school circuit and the malaise of bourgeois New Yorkers. It nailed the alienation of the young from the old, the pretentious from the real. But it remained a conventional novel—essentially a quest tale with an adolescent slant. It was *Nine Stories* that played with form and expectation, that bent the rules, that asked new questions about what fiction could do.

Salinger was also known as a writer in 1953 because many of his stories had been appearing in the *New Yorker* to some acclaim. After nearly a decade of rejection from the magazine, Salinger had a story accepted in 1946. "A Slight Rebellion off Madison"—which never made the cut for *Nine Stories*—featured Holden Caulfield, the adolescent narrator of *The Catcher in the Rye*, as a runaway. While that story generated some interest in Salinger, in 1948 his name generated a buzz at the *New Yorker*. He sold them three stories that year: "A Perfect Day for Bananafish" in January; "Uncle Wiggily in Connecticut" in March; and "Just Before the War with the Eskimos" in June. He'd received his New York benediction. It was a milestone, but also a step toward his permanent retreat from the East Coast literary scene.

By the time *Nine Stories* came out, Salinger had completed a writing apprenticeship that took him from penning stories, at age fifteen, on his dormitory bunk in the Valley Forge Military Academy in the Pennsylvania hills, to writing stories in the foxholes of WWII. He carried a typewriter in his army Jeep and by 1944 had published fiction in *Story*, *Collier's* and *The Saturday Evening Post*. His job as a soldier was to discover Gestapo agents by interviewing French civilians and captured Germans; he also landed at Normandy and took part in the Battle of the Bulge. While in Europe he had an audience with War Correspondent Hemingway, and later commented in a letter to his college friend Elizabeth Murray how little the man moved him. By the close of the war, he'd received several medals for valor but was deeply troubled.

In 1945, Salinger returned to the United States disillusioned and married, briefly, to a French doctor. (It was not the first time he'd experienced ruined love. Salinger, who grew up among the elite in prep schools and Manhattan's Upper West Side, had briefly dated Oona O'Neill, Eugene O'Neill's daughter, before she spurned him for Charlie Chaplin.) The marriage lasted eight months, and after the divorce Salinger began a period of drifting that lasted for several years. He left Manhattan, where he'd lived in his parents' Park Avenue apartment, for a garage apartment in Tarrytown, Westchester County, then to a barn studio in Stamford, Connecticut. While wandering, he read and studied Zen Buddhism and worked on new short stories. His fiction now moves from the high-concept punch of the *Collier's* mold, to the ephemeral quality that imbues *Nine Stories*.

During this time Salinger continued to work on *The Catcher in the Rye*, which was still finding momentum. In a set of Salinger archives at the Harry Ransom Center for Humanities in Texas are pages from a 1945 draft of

Catcher in which the narrative is in the third person. Holden Caulfield is there, center stage, but we don't see the world through his eyes. The manuscript pages seem flat without his jaded and wry inflection. This archive suggests that sometime during his post-war meandering pilgrimage, Salinger allowed Holden to take over the narrative and developed the alienated, adolescent voice that made the book famous.

Dislocated from his childhood New York, recuperating from the horrors of war, recently divorced, and deepening in his study of Zen, Salinger brought something new to his art. He developed two elements in his fiction—the austerity and submerged meaning found in *Nine Stories*, and the energized first-person narration found in his first and only novel. These additions ended up making his career.

*   *   *

When *Nine Stories* came out, it seemed to awe, puzzle, and unnerve reviewers in equal measure. The critics' response was partly determined by their ability to accept the stories as paradoxes rather than narrative statements. Eudora Welty reviewed *Nine Stories* in the *New York Times Book Review* on April 3, 1953. She wrote of Salinger, "He has the equipment of a born writer to begin with—his sensitive eye, his incredibly good ear, and something I think of no other word for but grace. There is not a trace of sentimentality in his work, although it is full of children that are bound to be adored." Paul Pickrel, in the *Yale Review*, calls one of the stories, "For Esmé—with Love and Squalor," "one of the greatest stories of the last decade, and technically one of the most dazzling I know." Seymour Krim, in *Commonweal*, compared Salinger to Fitzgerald: "both writers have that particular poignance which results from a lyrical identification with subject-matter set off by a critical intelligence; they are both lovers, so to speak, who are forced to acknowledge that they have been 'had,' and this gives their work the emotion of subtle heartbreak."

Among the detractors were Charles Poore, in the *New York Times*, and Sidney Monas, in the *Hudson Review*. Poore called the stories "disjointed, uneasy little dreams," while Monas wrote, "One has sometimes an oppressive and uncomfortable awareness of the author's nervous involvement in the hurt of his sensitive, witty, suicidal heroes. One also senses in these stories, as in the novel, a peculiar conceptual separation of the child from the adult, as though they were of different species, not merely different ages. For the child, anything is possible; for the adult, conformity or death."

While the critical response to Salinger's second book was mixed, the book received plenty of attention and sold well, despite the waning popularity of the American short story. People have continued to read it, keeping it reprinted in paperback for half a century. Exactly how many readers buy this book every year is unknown—book sales figures from the publishers, like everything Salinger-esque, are shrouded in secrecy.

*   *   *

The question of where Salinger fits in twentieth-century American literature is a complex one. Harold Bloom calls *Catcher in the Rye* and *Nine Stories* minor classics, and relates the former as "a Gatsby-like, modern version of Twain's *Huckleberry Finn*." The latter, these nine stories, often seem like fictional anomalies that arrived at the *New Yorker* in the middle of the last century. Salinger seems to borrow from multiple short story traditions and yet combines the elements into something that is uniquely his. The *Nine Stories* are clearly in the mold of the Chekhov-Hemingway school of dramatic realism—they attempt to compress action into fairly continuous segments of time; reveal character in-scene; and arrange fictional elements to give us the impression of lives stolen and submerged within the page. Exposition is rare and the stories, because of that, have a cinematic quality. Salinger's stories have the rich dialogue subtext of Hemingway stories, but the scenic treatment of *Nine Stories* is much more adorned, especially when it comes to character gesture, to the nuances of how a man holds a cigarette or folds a napkin. Salinger stories usually open at the heart of a crisis that is never fully explained. As David Stevenson, a Salinger critic, once remarked, "The Salinger–*New Yorker* story is always a kind of closet scene between Hamlet and his mother with the rest of the play left out."

In their use of the epiphany, the Salinger stories seem to merge Chekhov, Hemingway, and arch-modernist James Joyce. The crowning moments of *Nine Stories* have the gravity and significance one associates with Joyce stories like "Araby," but with the muted, barely reported, and subtle quality of certain Chekhov and Hemingway stories. The action resolution is extreme, but there is no narrator or writer to interpret its full meaning for us or the characters. We are left, as with the ending of "A Perfect Day for Bananafish," stunned and reeling, looking back through our reading for the fictional clues that support this outcome—the buried quips and ambiguous gestures that now seem ominous. Salinger's epiphanies are bold, then, but their significance emerges slowly in our minds, the images a little distorted; it's like we've watched the story's action through a pane of old, mottled glass. There is always an element of mystery and inscrutability.

It's not without irony that *Nine Stories* appears the same year as Cheever's *The Enormous Radio and Other Stories*. The two writers represent opposite reactions to the post-war era. Cheever captures the tide of wartime men returning to quiet neighborhoods to forget the horrors of combat; in such suburban enclaves the greatest moral failure is infidelity among married couples. The war must be forgotten. Salinger's stories seem to usher in an entirely different sentiment: the war has been internalized; men are broken and brutalized; corruption of the spirit can only occasionally be undone by the antidote of innocence, often in the form of children. Cheever finds some fundamental good in the return to the middle-class neighborhoods, in the solace of the nuclear family, while Salinger finds the worst kind of spiritual death in these same arenas. Salinger, by being ardently against conformity in all his fiction, amplifies his *Catcher in the Rye* theme of the individual estranged from society.

Nine Stories, then, in both theme and form, seems to hover in the middle of the last century as a strange and compelling amalgam of influences. These stories are a belated smorgasbord of certain modernist trends: they have the religious style epiphany of Joyce, the cinematic elegance of Chekhov, and some of the hard-boiled irony and deep subtext of Hemingway stories. To be sure, Salinger pales a little when laid against these masters, but he nonetheless encapsulates the bourgeois malaise and spiritual hunger of post-war America as opposed to the spirit of prosperity and return to suburban quietude that often characterizes fiction of this period. And he does this by expanding on the tradition of modernist fiction—the isolation of the individual from society takes on fresh angles and intensity, the structuring of meaning via juxtaposition instead of exposition is done elegantly, and the idea of a story as a puzzle becomes a crucial element. None of these things was individually new or novel in 1953, but the combination in Salinger's *Nine Stories* is particularly artful.

But "expanding on the tradition of modernism" does not fully capture the place of *Nine Stories* and Salinger in the roll call of twentieth-century short-story writers. That's because the unifying principle for Salinger is not so much a fictional aesthetic as it is a spiritual one: namely, Zen Buddhism. It is a curious coincidence of history that Zen and certain schools of modernism share a number of important ideas: life as illusory, life as suffering, non-attachment to fixed meaning, experience as fragmentary and subjective, intuition as central, a sense of the absurd in human experience, the necessity of irrationality combined with a turning away from absolute coherence and unity. Salinger, in applying his Zen orientation, happens to craft stories that are necessarily more oblique in their intentions than, say, Hemingway. For Salinger, character motivation is less important than the mystery of personality as revealed in the moment of crisis (while in good Hemingway stories there is often a strong logical sense of motivation in a character's actions). In bridging the demands of fiction with his Zen aesthetic, Salinger combines extreme epiphanies—Teddy falling into the swimming pool, Seymour shooting himself, the mother breaking down in "Uncle Wiggly in Connecticut"— with an extreme reliance on the present, dramatic moment. We don't pull out from the action and filter the epiphany through a changed state of consciousness as with Joyce's "Araby"; rather, we let the moment speak for itself. Zen as the unifying principle of Salinger's fiction after 1951 allows him to blend modernist techniques, to write between the poles of rationality and irrationality, meaning and randomness, character history and the exclusive reliance on the "witnessed" moment. The mysterious inner lives of his characters, the labyrinth of character and story through which he minimally guides us, that slight sensation that we have missed some vital clue to a character's downfall yet recognize that this is the same clue we miss every time we watch the disasters of the evening news or a neighbor's life reduced to tragedy—these arise out of navigating between these poles and become Salinger's fictional legacy. Fifty years on, Salinger's *Nine Stories* remain compelling anomalies.

*   *   *

Nowhere has Salinger endured more, especially with *Nine Stories*, than among younger American writers. In a book co-edited with Thomas Beller—*With Love and Squalor*—Kip Kotzen suggests that "writers have a different, very sensitive, sometimes quite introspective view of the world that Salinger captured in his work." In this book, fourteen writers, including Charles D'Ambrosio, Aleksander Hemon, and Aimee Bender, respond to Salinger and his work with personal essays. While they differ in their appreciation of his art, all agree that Salinger did something important to fiction, particularly to the short story, in the second half of the twentieth century. There is a sense among many of these younger writers that Salinger is to them what Twain and Dickens were to aspiring writers a century ago.

For writer René Steinke, *Nine Stories* encapsulated an era of musing about the wider world as a thirteen-year-old girl in a small Texas town: "Salinger's deceptively straightforward sentences seemed to sing to me; the searching observations, not unlike the kind I had when I was bored or daydreaming, felt familiar. There were compact, memorable lines, part smart-aleck, part philosophical, that struck me as unpretentious and wise. It was clearly an adult book, but if felt as if it had been written for me." Steinke goes on to recount a story told by a New York uncle in which there were "excited people lining up around the block, the way people now line up for concert tickets, waiting at the newsstand to buy the new *New Yorker* with the latest Salinger story printed inside."

Today, the image of fans lining up for magazine fiction seems surreal—something dredged from a writer's ego-dream. And it's equally puzzling to imagine a writer walking away from that amount of fame. But walk he did, from the Greenwich literary haunts to the ninety-acre wood in New Hampshire. He slipped away from us and we should have seen it coming—all the clues were in *Nine Stories*. While his retreat was surely coming into focus even as *Catcher in the Rye* was still selling in hardback, there is a way in which *Nine Stories* holds the key to Salinger's upcoming escape. The stories cement the theme that Salinger introduced in the novel and that resonated in his own life: the sensitive, alienated man in search of innocence and love in a world of corruption. In other words, a man who wants to escape the "phonies."

But the search for this innocence leads to exile. And here is the point where Salinger's biography intersects with his fiction most profoundly. Whereas writers like Nabokov used exile from the homeland as a catalyst for expression, Salinger created exile for himself and his characters. The writer gets lost in his New Hampshire hermitage, just as his child heroes are marooned by their quest for innocence, or by being too gifted or too sensitive. Paradoxically—this is the fiction of Zen after all—these same children are Salinger's symbols of hope.

But hope, when it comes in *Nine Stories*, is not just in the form of the grand epiphany. It comes in the little things: a girl's appreciation of wax and olives, her tactile pleasure with sand; Esmé's conversational lilt and her brother's love of riddles; a boy's thrill over a story told on a snowy night concerning kidnapping Chinese bandits; the small pleasure of Teddy, the boy genius, keeping lists in his pockets of things to look up at the library—these are the big ticket items in Salinger's fictional universe. These are the moments that make the exile worthwhile.

Whether *Nine Stories* will, in fact, prove to be the high point of Salinger's literary career remains to be seen. The *New Yorker* stories that came after it—"Franny" (1955), "Raise High the Roof Beam, Carpenters" (1955), "Zooey" (1957), "Seymour: An Introduction" (1959), and "Hapworth 16, 1924" (1965), while containing moments of brilliance, were a little too self-conscious and rambling, and they floundered between forms. They lacked the distilled power of good short stories and the full-bellied story arcs of superior novels. But Salinger has continued to write for at least some of these last four decades of publishing silence, or so we're told. In both the Joyce Maynard memoir (*At Home in the World*) and the Margaret Salinger autobiography (*Dream Catcher*) the authors report that Salinger has been writing every day, keeping his developing opus in a safe. In the 1990s, when Salinger sued his unauthorized biographer, Ian Hamilton, over alleged misuse of Salinger's unpublished letters, the writer stated, under oath, that he had been continuing to write all these years. But when asked by the court what kind of writing he does, he hesitated, saying that it was very difficult to define his current project. No one can be sure what he's been working on; it sounds as if even he is not sure. A continuation of the Glass Family saga? A novel narrated by the Zen saint Seymour Glass before his untimely death? Possibly. In a letter written to longtime friend Elizabeth Murray in 1963, Salinger indicates that he has a long way to go before finishing with the Glass family. But then that strange and long story, "Hapworth 16, 1924," which includes a letter from the young Seymour Glass at summer camp, came along and tried to tie up the loose ends of the family's fictional life. That long, disjointed story was Salinger's last published word.

If a novel or a set of stories emerges from Salinger's posthumous vault in Cornish, New Hampshire, it will undoubtedly arouse a great deal of literary interest. But as interesting as that outcome might be, the question of whether Salinger's craft benefited from his long-standing and self-imposed exile is a striking one. One hopes he made a return to the austerity and submerged tension of *Nine Stories*. As the book turns fifty, it seems more than ever that this is where Salinger's art and life intersected best. Personal turmoil, spiritual hunger, and the sheer prowess of Salinger's literary craft, all combined to make this collection the best sort of Zen koan—one that's pleasing and unforgettable in its own right.

Chronology

1919	Jerome David Salinger, the second of two children, is born in New York City on January 1, to Sol and Miriam Jillich Salinger.
1936	Graduates from Valley Forge Military Academy in Pennsylvania.
1938	Travels in Europe.
1939	Attends a short story writing course taught by Whit Burnett at Columbia University. His first short story, "The Young Folks," is published the following year in Burnett's magazine *Story*.
1942	Drafted into United States Army and attends Officers, First Sergeants, and Instructors School of the Signal Corps.
1943	Stationed in Nashville, Tennessee, then transferred to the Army Counter-Intelligence Corps. His short story "The Varioni Brothers" is published in the *Saturday Evening Post*.
1944	Sent to Europe, assigned to the Fourth Division of the U.S. Army, and later lands at Utah Beach as a part of the D-Day invasion force. Participates in European campaigns as security agent for the Twelfth Infantry Regiment.
1945–47	In 1945, hospitalized for "battle fatigue." Discharged from Army in 1945 and begins to publish regularly in the *Saturday Evening Post*, *Esquire*, and the *New Yorker*.
1948–50	Begins long publishing relationship with the *New Yorker*. Publishes the major short stories "A Perfect Day for Bananafish,"

"Uncle Wiggily in Connecticut," "Just Before the War with the Eskimos," "The Laughing Man," and "For Esmé—with Love and Squalor" in the *New Yorker* during these years.

1950   Film version of "Uncle Wiggily in Connecticut," *My Foolish Heart*, is released by Samuel Goldwyn and stars Susan Hayward and Dana Andrews.

1951   *The Catcher in the Rye* is published. "Pretty Mouth and Green My Eyes" published in the *New Yorker*.

1953   Moves to Cornish, New Hampshire. "Teddy" published in the *New Yorker*. *Nine Stories* published in April.

1955   Marries Claire Douglas on February 17. "Raise High the Roof Beam, Carpenters" and "Franny" published in the *New Yorker*. Daughter, Margaret Ann, born on December 10.

1957–59   "Zooey" and "Seymour: An Introduction" are published in the *New Yorker*.

1960   Son Matthew is born on February 13.

1961   *Franny and Zooey* published.

1963   *Raise High the Roof Beam, Carpenters* and *Seymour: An Introduction* published.

1965   "Hapworth 16, 1924" published in the *New Yorker*.

1967   Divorced.

1974   Denounces the unauthorized *Complete Uncollected Short Stories of J. D. Salinger* in his only public statement in many years.

1987   Publication of Ian Hamilton's biography, *J. D. Salinger: A Writing Life*, is prohibited because quotations from Salinger's letters violate his copyright.

1988   Last published short story, "Hapworth 16, 1924," released in book form. Ian Hamilton publishes *In Search of J. D. Salinger*, which omits all references to Salinger's letters.

2010   Dies at home in January.

Contributors

HAROLD BLOOM is Sterling Professor of the Humanities at Yale University. Educated at Cornell and Yale universities, he is the author of more than 30 books, including *Shelley's Mythmaking* (1959), *Blake's Apocalypse* (1963), *Yeats* (1970), *The Anxiety of Influence* (1973), *A Map of Misreading* (1975), *Kabbalah and Criticism* (1975), *Agon: Toward a Theory of Revisionism* (1982), *The American Religion* (1992), *The Western Canon* (1994), *Omens of Millennium: The Gnosis of Angels, Dreams, and Resurrection* (1996), *Shakespeare: The Invention of the Human* (1998), *How to Read and Why* (2000), *Genius: A Mosaic of One Hundred Exemplary Creative Minds* (2002), *Hamlet: Poem Unlimited* (2003), *Where Shall Wisdom Be Found?* (2004), *Jesus and Yahweh: The Names Divine* (2005), and *Till I End My Song: A Gathering of Last Poems* (2010). In addition, he is the author of hundreds of articles, reviews, and editorial introductions. In 1999, Professor Bloom received the American Academy of Arts and Letters' Gold Medal for Criticism. He has also received the International Prize of Catalonia, the Alfonso Reyes Prize of Mexico, and the Hans Christian Andersen Bicentennial Prize of Denmark.

GORDON E. SLETHAUG has been chairman of the program in American studies at the University of Hong Kong. He is the author of *The Play of the Double in Postmodern American Fiction* and *Beautiful Chaos: Chaos Theory and Metachaotics in Recent American Fiction.*

GARY LANE has taught at the University of Michigan. He has published concordances to the poetry of Ezra Pound and Hart Crane and *Sylvia Plath: New Views on the Poetry.*

JAMES LUNDQUIST has published on Kurt Vonnegut, Jack London, Sinclair Lewis, and others.

RICHARD ALLAN DAVISON is a retired professor of the English department at the University of Delaware. He has written books on Charles Norris and Charles and Kathleen Norris, and he is a coeditor of *The Actor's Art: Conversations With Contemporary American Stage Performers*.

JOHN WENKE is a professor at Salisbury State University. He has published *J.D. Salinger: A Study of the Short Fiction* and *Melville's Muse: Literary Creation and the Forms of Philosophical Fiction*.

DENNIS L. O'CONNOR has been a writer and editor. His collection of experimental fiction is *Reconsider*, and he has worked on a book on Salinger's Glass family stories.

ANTHONY KAUFMAN is a professor emeritus at the University of Illinois. He is the editor of *Steven Soderbergh: Interviews*.

EBERHARD ALSEN is a retired professor of the State University of New York, Cortland. His publications include *A Reader's Guide to J. D. Salinger* and *Salinger's Glass Stories as a Composite Novel*.

DOMINIC SMITH serves on the fiction faculty in the Warren Wilson MFA Program for Writers. He is the author of the novels *The Mercury Visions of Louis Daguerre* and *The Beautiful Miscellaneous*.

Bibliography

Alsen, Eberhard. *A Reader's Guide to J.D. Salinger.* Westport, Conn.; London: Greenwood Press, 2002.

———. *Salinger's Glass Stories as a Composite Novel.* Troy, N.Y.: Whitston, 1983.

Ames, Melissa. "Memoirs of a Bathroom Stall: The Women's Lavatory as Crying Room, Confessional, & Sanctuary." *EAPSU Online: A Journal of Critical and Creative Work* 3 (Fall 2006): 63–74.

Antico, John. "The Parody of J. D. Salinger: Esmé and the Fat Lady Exposed." *Modern Fiction Studies* 12 (Fall 1966): 325–40.

Bawer, Bruce. "Salinger's Arrested Development." *The New Criterion* 5, no. 1 (September 1986): 34–47.

Belcher, William F., and James W. Lee, ed. *J. D. Salinger and the Critics.* Belmont, Calif.: Wadsworth, 1962.

Bloom, Harold, ed. *J. D. Salinger.* New York: Infobase Publishing, 2008.

Boe, Alfred F. "Street Games in J. D. Salinger and Gerald Green." *Modern Fiction Studies* 33, no. 1 (Spring 1987): 65–72.

Bryan, James E. "J. D. Salinger: The Fat Lady and the Chicken Sandwich." *College English* 23, no. 3 (December 1961): 226–9.

———. "A Reading of Salinger's 'For Esmé—with Love and Squalor.'" *Criticism: A Quarterly for Literature and the Arts* 9 (1967): 275–88.

Crawford, Catherine, ed. *If You Really Want to Hear About It: Writers on J.D. Salinger and His Work.* New York: Thunder's Mouth Press, 2006.

Davis, Tom. "J. D. Salinger: 'The Sound of One Hand Clapping.'" *Wisconsin Studies in Contemporary Literature* 4, no. 1 (Winter 1963): 41–7.

129

Emerson, Gloria. "The Children in the Field." *TriQuarterly* 65 (Winter 1986): 221–8.

French, Warren. *J. D. Salinger.* Rev. ed. Boston: Twayne, 1976.

———. *J. D. Salinger, Revisited.* Boston: Twayne, 1988.

Galloway, David D. *The Absurd Hero in American Fiction: Updike, Styron, Bellow, Salinger.* Austin: University of Texas Press, 1970.

Goldstein, Bernice. "'Seymour: An Introduction'—Writing as Discovery." *Studies in Short Fiction* 7 (1970): 248–56.

———. "Seymour's Poems." *Literature East and West* 17 (1973): 335–48.

———. "Zen and Nine Stories." *Renascence: Essays on Value in Literature* 22 (1970): 171–82.

Goldstein, Bernice, and Sanford Goldstein. "Ego and 'Hapworth 16, 1924.'" *Renascence: Essays on Value in Literature* 24 (1972): 159–67.

Goldstein, Sanford. "Some Zen References in Salinger." *Literature East and West* 15 (1971): 83–95.

Grunwald, Henry Anatole, ed. *Salinger: A Critical and Personal Portrait.* New York: Harper & Row, 1963, 1962.

Hamilton, Kenneth. *J. D. Salinger, a Critical Essay.* Grand Rapids, Mich.: Eerdmans, 1967.

Harper, Howard M., Jr. *Desperate Faith: A Study of Bellow, Salinger, Mailer, Baldwin, and Updike.* Chapel Hill: University of North Carolina Press, 1967.

Hassan, Ihab. "Almost the Voice of Silence: The Later Novelettes of J. D. Salinger." *Wisconsin Studies in Contemporary Literature* 4, no. 1 (Winter 1963): 5–20.

———. "J. D. Salinger: Rare Quixotic Gesture." *Western Review* 21 (1957): 261–80.

Karlstetter, Karl. "J.D. Salinger, R. W. Emerson and the Perennial Philosophy." *Moderna Sprak* 63 (1969): 224–36.

Kirschner, Paul. "Salinger and His Society: The Pattern of Nine Stories." *Literary Half-Yearly* 14, no. 2 (1973): 63–78.

———. "Salinger and Scott Fitzgerald: Complementary American Voices." *Dutch Quarterly Review of Anglo-American Letters* 17, no. 1 (1987): 53–73.

Korte, Barbara. "Narrative Perspective in the Works of J. D. Salinger." *Literatur in Wissenschaft und Unterricht* 20, no. 2 (1987): 343–51.

Kotzen, Kip, and Thomas Beller, ed. *With Love and Squalor: 14 Writers Respond to the Work of J. D. Salinger.* New York: Broadway Books, 2001.

Laser, Marvin, and Norman Fruman, ed. *Studies in J. D. Salinger: Reviews, Essays, and Critiques of* The Catcher in the Rye, *and Other Fiction.* New York: Odyssey Press, 1963.

McSweeney, Kerry. "Salinger Revisited." *Critical Quarterly* 20, no. 1 (1978): 61–8.

Miller, James E., Jr. *J. D. Salinger.* Minneapolis: University of Minnesota Press, 1965.

Phillips, Paul. "Salinger's *Franny and Zooey*." *Mainstream: A Literary Quarterly* 25, no. 1 (1962): 32–9.

Purcell, William F. "World War II and the Early Fiction of J. D. Salinger." *Studies in American Literature* 28 (1991): 77–93.

Razdan, Brij M. "From Unreality to Reality: *Franny and Zooey*, A Reinterpretation." *Panjab University Research Bulletin* 9, nos. 1–2 (April–October 1978): 3–15.

Rose, Alan H. "Sin and the City: The Uses of Disorder in the Urban Novel." *Centennial Review* 16 (1972): 203–20.

Rosen, Gerald. *Zen in the Art of J. D. Salinger*. Berkeley: Creative Arts, 1977.

Santos, Sherod. "Poetry and Attention: J. D. Salinger, Agassiz and the Fish, and a Paper Sack of Ripe Tomatoes." *New England Review and Bread Loaf Quarterly* 9, no. 3 (Spring 1987): 348–56.

Slethaug, Gordon E. "Form in Salinger's Shorter Fiction." *Canadian Review of American Studies* 3 (1972): 50–9.

Sørensen, Brent. *Youth and Innocence as Textual Constructs in the Short Stories of J. D. Salinger and Douglas Coupland*. Odense: Center for American Studies, University of Southern Denmark, 2004.

Strong, Paul. "Black Wing, Black Heart—Betrayal in J. D. Salinger's 'The Laughing Man.'" *West Virginia University Philological Papers* 31 (1986): 91–6.

Tae, Yasuhiro. "Between Suicide and Enlightenment." *Kyushu American Literature* 26 (October 1985): 21–7.

Takenaka, Toyoko. "On Seymour's Suicide." *Kyushu American Literature* 12 (1970): 54–61.

Weber, Myles. *Consuming Silences: How We Read Authors Who Don't Publish*. Athens: University of Georgia Press, 2005.

Wenke, John. *J. D. Salinger: A Study of the Short Fiction*. Boston: Twayne, 1991.

Wexelblatt, Robert. "Chekhov, Salinger, and Epictetus." *Midwest Quarterly: A Journal of Contemporary Thought* 28, no. 1 (Autumn 1986): 50–76.

Acknowledgments

Gordon E. Slethaug, "Seymour: A Clarification." From *Renascence: Essays on Values in Literature* 23, no. 4 (Summer 1971): 115–28. Copyright © 1971 by *Renascence*.

Gary Lane, "Seymour's Suicide Again: A New Reading of J. D. Salinger's 'A Perfect Day for Bananafish.'" From *Studies in Short Fiction* 10, no. 1 (Winter 1973): 27–34. Copyright © 1973 by Newberry College.

James Lundquist, "A Cloister of Reality: The Glass Family." From *J. D. Salinger*, pp. 115–50, 160–62. Copyright © 1979 by Frederick Ungar Publishing.

Richard Allan Davison, "Salinger Criticism and 'The Laughing Man': A Case of Arrested Development." From *Studies in Short Fiction* 18, no. 1 (Winter 1981): 1–15. Copyright © 1981 by Newberry College; afterword © 2011 by Richard Allan Davison.

John Wenke, "Sergeant X, Esmé, and the Meaning of Words." From *Studies in Short Fiction* 18, no. 3 (Summer 1981): 251–59. Copyright © 1981 by Newberry College.

Dennis L. O'Connor, "J. D. Salinger's Religious Pluralism: The Example of *Raise High the Roof Beam, Carpenters.*" From *The Southern Review* 20, no. 2 (April 1984): 316–32. Copyright © 1984 by Dennis O'Connor.

Anthony Kaufman, "'Along this road goes no one': Salinger's 'Teddy' and the Failure of Love." From *Studies in Short Fiction* 35 (1998): 129–40. Copyright © 1998 by Newberry College.

Eberhard Alsen, "New Light on the Nervous Breakdowns of Salinger's Sergeant X and Seymour Glass." From *CLA Journal* 45, no. 2 (March 2002): 379–87. Copyright © 2002 by the College Language Association.

Dominic Smith, "Salinger's *Nine Stories:* Fifty Years Later." From *The Antioch Review* 61, no. 4 (Fall 2003): 639–49. Copyright © 2003 by Dominic Smith.

Index

Characters in literary works are indexed by first name (if any), followed by the name of the work in parentheses

agape, defined, 15
Alsen, Eberhard, 53–54, 65n7
American Literary Scholarship (Stafford), 54
"Araby" (Joyce), 122

Battle of the Bulge, 110
Beatrice Glass (Boo Boo), 5–6, 30–31
Beckett, Samuel, 35
Belcher, William E., 56
Belle, Thomas, 122
Bellow, Saul, 55
Bender, Aimee, 122
Bessie Glass (Franny and Zooey), 30–31
Bloom, Harold, 120
Blotner, Joseph, 54
blue color, significance of, 15, 18
Boo Boo ("Raise High the Roof Beam, Carpenters"), 93–94
Boo Boo Glass ("Down at the Dinghy"), 30
Booper ("Teddy"), 97, 98, 100–101
Bradstreet, Ken, 110
Bramble, Pete, 109
Buddhist intuition, 92
Buddy Glass (Franny"), as home movie, 36

Buddy Glass ("Raise High the Roof Beam, Carpenters")
  and glass significance, 46
  and Heavenly Way, 89
  on religious pluralism, 80
  on Seymour's poetry, 17
Buddy Glass ("Seymour—An Introduction")
  and compromise monologue, 46–47
  and divine insight, 12
  and religious insight, 11
  on Seymour's hands, 13
  on Seymour's "madness of the heart," 9
  and "Teddy," 95, 105n1
  on touching, 14
Burnett, Whit, 30

Camus, Albert, 35
Catcher in the Rye, The
  Bloom on, 120
  as conventional novel, 117–118
  draft in Salinger archives (1945), 117–118
  popularity of, 116, 117
  publication of, 116
  Salinger "exile" and, 123

theme of, 121
Chang Chung-yuan, 84
"Charlotte," 13
Cheever, John, 114, 120–121
Christian Century, The, 42
Christianity, 20, 40, 41
Chuang-Tzu, 84, 85, 86–87
Clay ("For Esmé—with Love and
    Squalor"), 71–72, 74, 76
concentration camps, 110
Creativity and Taoism (Chang
    Chung-yuan), 84
critical reaction to Salinger
    book-length studies of Salinger,
        53–54
    decline of critical interest, 53,
        65n1, 69
    "For Esmé—with Love and
        Squalor," 74
    Franny and Zooey, 41–42
    "Hapworth 16, 1924," 51
    "The Laughing Man," 55–57
    Nine Stories, 119–120
    "Raise High the Roof Beam,
        Carpenters," 49–50, 51
    "Seymour—An Introduction,"
        49–50, 51

D'Ambrosio, Charles, 122
"De Daumier-Smith's Blue Period,"
    29, 55
"Down at the Dinghy," 5, 30, 55, 64
Doyle, James P., 53–54
Dream Catcher (M. Salinger), 107
Duino Elegies (Rilke), 22–23, 33

Eliot, T.S., 22, 79
Emerson, Ralph Waldo, 11–12, 79
Emerson's Perennial Philosophy, 35
Enormous Radio and Other Stories,
    The (Cheever), 116–117, 120

Fall, The (Camus), 35
fate, 18
feet, emphasis on childlike, 15, 18

Fiedler, Leslie, 74
Fiene, Donald M., 56
first-person narrators, 57, 119
Fitzgerald, F. Scott, 33, 45–46, 62,
    119
"For Esmé—with Love and Squalor"
    autobiographical story, 110
    best short story, 69, 76, 119
    conclusion of, 75–77
    critical debate over in fifties and
        sixties, 70, 77n1
    extreme human misery and, 72
    letter from Esmé, 74
    malaprops and, 73
    "modern epithalamium," 76, 77n4
    plot of, 116
    significance in Salinger fiction,
        72
    and tea room conversation, 73–74
Fosburgh, Lacey, 112
Fourth Elegy (Rilke), 23
"Franny," 5–6
Franny ("Franny"), touching of
    forehead, 14
Franny (Franny and Zooey),
    and Taoist ideal of yielding
    formlessness, 85
Franny ("Zooey"), antiacademic
    comment of, 16
Franny and Zooey, 32, 33, 40–41,
    42, 47
Franny Glass (Franny and Zooey),
    33–34, 37, 39
French, Warren, 53, 57, 96
Fruman, Norman, 56

Giles, Lionel, 80
"Girl I Knew, A," 110
Glass family saga
    See also individual family names
Glass family structure
    affection and inspiration, 14
    Beatrice (Boo Boo) Glass (oldest
        girl), 31
    Bessie Glass (mother), 6, 30–31

Buddy Glass (Salinger's alter ego), 31
Franny (youngest), 6, 32
Les Glass (father), 6, 30–31
Seymour Glass (oldest), 31
Tannenbaum (Boo Boo's husband), 31
Waker and Walt (twins), 31–32
Zachary Martan Glass (Zooey) (actor), 6, 32
"Granny" ("A Perfect Day for Bananafish"), 6, 8
Great Gatsby, The (Fitzgerald), 45–46
Grunwald, Henry Anatole, 56

Hagen, Philip E., 56
Hamilton, Ian, 123
"Hapworth 16, 1924"
    last published work of Salinger, 124
    Mr. Happy and, 10
    plot of, 50–51
    publication of, 5, 50, 53, 65n2
    See also Seymour Glass ("Hapworth 16, 1924")
Harry Ransom Center for Humanities in Texas, 118
Hartwig, Robert T., 109
Hassan, Ihab, 50, 56, 76
Heavenly Way, Taoist teaching of, 89
Hellcats (Bradstreet), 110
Hemingway, Ernest, 107, 115
Hemon, Aleksander, 122
Hicks, Granville, 42
Holden Caulfield (The Catcher in the Rye), 32
Holden Caulfield "A Slight Rebellion off Madison," 118
homosexuality, latent, 7, 13–14, 17, 43, 89
Hotchner, A.E., 116
Howe, Irving, 49
Hurlach, Bavaria., 108–109

Hyman, Stanley Edgar, 51

If You Really Want To Know: A Catcher Casebook (Marsden), 56
In Our Time (Hemingway), 115
"It's a Wise Child" (children's quiz program), 6, 15, 32, 38, 40, 85

James, Henry, 29
J. D. Salinger (French), 57
J. D. Salinger (Miller), 54
J. D. Salinger and the Critics (Lee), 56, 66n30
J. D. Salinger Special Number of Modern Fiction Studies, 57
Jesus Prayer, 34–35, 38, 69
John Gedsudski ("The Laughing Man")
    balking at adult commitment, 63–64, 65
    complexities of, 59–60
    French on, 57
    and metaphor of Laughing Man, 60–61
    naiveté toward sex, 59
Johnson, Gerden F., 108
Joyce, James, 122
"Just Before the War with the Eskimos," 55, 64, 116–117, 118
Justice, James H., 54

Kafka quotation, 47
Kao ("Raise High the Roof Beam, Carpenters"), 82, 87
Kaufering Lager IV, 109
Kazin, Alfred, 41–42
Kierkegaard quotation, 47–48
Kotzen, Kip, 122
Krim, Seymour, 119

Land ("Franny"), 8
Lane Coutell (Franny and Zooey), 33
Laser, Marvin, 56
"Laughing Man, The"

and adult insights, 64
analysis of, 57–60
baby carriage motif, 59, 67n46
critical commentary on, 55–57
and fair play, 60–61, 67n48
final encounter of Laughing Man
    with DuFarges, 61
hypocrisy of Laughing Man's
    parents, 61, 67n50
lack of attention to, 55
point of view of, 57–58
semiparody on college athlete-
    hero, 62
Lee, James W., 56
legacy of Salinger
    basis of reputation, 95
    escaping the "phonies," 123
    fiction remains compelling
        anomalies, 122
    "Hapworth 16, 1924" last
        published work, 124
    introspective view of world, 122
    place in twentieth-century
        American literature, 120
    possibility of posthumous
        writings, 124
    self-imposed exile, 123
    smorgasbord of modernist trends,
        121
    spiritual hunger of postwar
        America, 121
    and Zen Buddhism, 121–122
Lehan, Richard D., 54
Levine, Paul, 49–50
Lieh-tzu's parable, 81
Loretta ("For Esmé—with Love and
    Squalor"), 71–72
Lu Chi-p'u, 86

Malamud, Bernard, 55
Malmedy, Belgium, 110
Marsden, Malcolm, 56
Mary Hudson ("The Laughing
    Man")
    ambivalence of, 59

breakup with Gedsudski, 57
picture of, 58, 66n41
as unattainable society girl, 62
Mayhew, A.E., 41–42
Maynard, Joyce, 123
Merton, Thomas, 79
Miller, James E., 54
Mi Yujen, 84
Modern Language Association
    session on Salinger, 54
Monas, Sidney, 119
Mr. and Mrs. McArdle ("Teddy"),
    99–100
Mrs. Fedder ("Raise High the Roof
    Beam, Carpenters"), 6–7, 9
Mueller, Max, 36
Muriel Fedder ("Raise High the
    Roof Beam, Carpenters"), 93–94
Muriel Fedder Glass ("A Perfect Day
    for Bananafish"), 6, 7, 18
Murray, Elizabeth, 118, 124

Nameless One ("Raise High the
    Roof Beam, Carpenters")
    cigar as symbol, 91–92
    divine quality of, 88
    kinship with Seymour, 89
    Tathagata and, 92
    transcends classification, 85–87
New Yorker, The, 32, 42, 50, 53, 53,
    61, 79, 117, 118, 120, 122, 123
New York Times Book Review, 41,
    49, 119
Nicholson ("Teddy"), 100–102
Nine Stories
    austerity and submerged meaning
        in, 119
    begins and ends with suicide, 98,
        105n5
    bold epiphanies in, 120
    Chekhov, Hemingway, and Joyce
        merged, 120
    mold of Chekhov-Hemingway,
        120
    popularity of, 119–120

publication of, 115–116
Seymour's suicide and, 5–6
"Teddy" and, 30, 95–96
thematic extremes of, 116–117
thematic unity of, 97
writing progression in, 29–30
Zen koan instead of author
    photo, 117
See also legacy of Salinger
Nirvana, 92

O'Connor, Dennis L., 53–54, 65n7
O'Connor, Flannery, 55, 117
O'Connor, Margaret Ann, 55
O'Neill, Oona, 118

Peale, Norman Vincent, satire on, 10
"Perfect Day for Bananafish, A"
    New Yorker and, 118
    parables in, 5–6
    popularity of, 54
Philokalia, The, 91
Pickrel, Paul, 119
Pilgrim Continues His Way, The, 11
Poore, Charles, 119
"Pretty Mouth and Green My Eyes,"
    55, 64

"Raise High the Roof Beam,
    Carpenters"
    first story with Glass family, 5–6
    Lieh-tzu's parable, 81
    publication of, 42, 79
    religious dimensions of, 79
    and Seymour's wedding, 14–15,
        43–46
    sheet paper symbolism and, 93,
        94
    Taoist background of, 80
    Taoist fellowship and, 82
"Rare Quixotic Gesture, The"
    (Hassan), 56
Rilke, Rainer Maria, 26n6, 33, 52n4
Roderick Hudson (James), 29
Roth, Phillip, 55

Rubin, Louis D., 54

Sacred Books of the East (Mueller),
    36
Salinger, A Critical and Personal
    Portrait (Grunwald), 56
Salinger, J.D.
    and Hemingway, 107, 118
    life after World War II, 118–119
    national literary figure, 116
    and nervous breakdown, 108, 111
    reclusiveness of, 116, 123
    waning popularity of, 53–55
    writing apprenticeship of, 118
    and World war II, 108, 111, 118
    See also legacy of Salinger
Salinger, Margaret (daughter), 106,
    111, 123
"Salinger Industry, The" (Steiner),
    56
Salinger's Catcher in the Rye:
    Clamor vs Criticism (Simonson
    and Hagen), 56
Saturday Evening Post, The, 12
Saturday Review, The, 42
Seiller, Edward F., 109
Sergeant X ("For Esmé—with Love
    and Squalor")
    and brother's letter, 74–75
    nervous breakdown of, 111, 112
    redemption of, 70
    sarcasm and sincerity fluctuation,
        73
    and two women in his life, 70–71
    use of cliché, 71
"Seymour—An Introduction," 5,
    42–43
    See also Buddy Glass
        ("Seymour—An Introduction")
Seymour Glass
    and innocence, 18
    as poet, 14
    sensuality over spirituality, 17
Seymour Glass ("A Perfect Day for
    Bananafish")

artistic sensitivity of, 7
considered a freak, 98–99
"controlled accident" and, 48
insanity of, 7, 8, 9–10, 19
Jewish-Irish background of, 10
and limited time in appearance,
11, 20n5
name significance, 25
parable of defeat is decision for
death, 25–26
possible former patient in
psychiatric ward of army
hospital, 111–112
preoccupation with death, 99
suicide of, 5, 6, 7, 18–19, 31, 99
Seymour Glass ("Hapworth 16,
1924")
on beautiful things, 12
childlike love of, 15
and Christian concept of agape,
15
delight in life, 14
and fate, 18–19
on originality, 16
on seeing, 11–12
Seymour Glass ("Raise High the
Roof Beam, Carpenters")
crying from happiness, 15
"dead cat" remark, 44
diary entry before wedding, 83
as Gatsby figure, 45–46
mysterious equanimity of, 83–84
on poetry, 16
Taoist fellowship and, 82
on touching, 13
wedding, 14–15, 43–46, 83
Sharon Lipschutz ("A Perfect Day
for Bananafish"), 7, 18, 24
short story form, Salinger and, 30
Simonson Harold P., 56
Simon Wiesenthal Multimedia
Learning Center, 110
Singe, I.B., 55
"Slight Rebellion off Madison, A,"
118

smoking, characters' addiction to,
12–13
Sonny Varioni ("The Varioni
Brothers"), hearing music, 12
Steiner, George, 56
Steinke, René, 122
Stevens, Wallace, 25
Stevenson, David, 120
Studies in J. D. Salinger (Laser and
Fruman), 56
style of Salinger
and "For Esmé," 76
as internal monologue, 30
Orientalism, 79
religious pluralism and, 91
and short story form, 30
"wait" rather than "quest," 35
Sybil ("A Perfect Day for
Bananafish")
linking of Sybil to Sharon and
Waste Land, 27n9
Seymour and, 7–8, 18, 23–24
as tarnishing symbol of human
condition, 25

Tannenbaum (Boo Boo's husband),
31
Taoist Teachings from the Book of
Lieh-tzu (Giles), 80
Tao Te Ching of Lao Tzu, 81
"Teddy"
first scene of, 99–100
and redemptive love doctrine, 104
Salinger's critique of, 95
significance to Nine Stories,
104–105
Teddy ("Teddy")
and adult insights, 64
haiku written before death, 101
as mystic, 10, 95–96, 105n2
and poison, 97, 105n3
response to parents, 101–102
sexual anxiety of, 102–103, 106n8
similarities to Seymour, 97,
105n4, 105n7

suicide of, 97, 98, 102, 103, 105n6
as unloved, 97, 101
themes of Salinger
dissolution of opposites, 35
ego loss, 35
individual estranged from society, 121
religious mysticism, 38
uneasiness with sexuality, 103, 106n8
See also Zen Buddhism
The Way of a Pilgrim, 34
Thoreau, Henry David, 11–12, 79
touching in Salinger, 13–14
transcendentalists, 11–12, 14, 20n6, 79
transmigration of the soul, Glass family and, 10, 19n4

"Uncle Wiggily in Connecticut"
publication of, 118
subject matter of, 64
and Walt in World War II, 30, 32, 117
Updike, John, 41

Valley Forge Military Academy, 118
"Varioni Brothers, The," 12

Wain, John, 49

Waiting for Godot (Beckett), 35
Walker and Walt Glass (twins), 6, 31–32
Walt Glass ("Uncle Wiggily in Connecticut"), 30
Warren, Robert Penn, 54
Waste Land, The (Eliot), 22, 24
Weinberg, Helen, 47
Welty, Eudora, 119
Wiegand, William, 56
With Love and Squalor (Beller and Kotzen), 122

Zachary Martin Glass (aka Zooey), 32
Zen Buddhism, 30, 38, 40–41, 45, 119, 121–122
Zen koan, defined, 117
Zen neophyte, 35
Zooey (Franny and Zooey)
on family's religion, 41
and Franny, 39–40
and Taoist ideal of yielding formlessness, 85
ulcer developed by, 39
Zooey ("Zooey")
actor, 6
on knowledge uses, 16–17
on psychoanalysts, 8–9
ulcer developed by, 37–38